THINK

THINK

The Foundation of Self-Awareness and Engagement

J. Ibeh Agbanyim
and
Raveen Arora

John Westley Publishing

THINK: The Foundation of Self-Awareness and Engagement

J. Ibeh Agbanyim: http://www.fvgrowth.com, *or email:* powerofengagement@att.net
Raveen Arora: http://www.thinkhuman.us, *or email,* arora.raveen@gmail.com

Because of the dynamic nature of the Internet, any web addresses or links contained in this book may have changed since publication and may no longer be valid. The views expressed in this work are solely those of the author and do not necessarily reflect the views of the publisher, and the publisher hereby disclaims any responsibility for them.

Printed in the United States of America
John Westley Publishing

ISBN: 978-0-9976801-3-3

ISBN: 978-0-9976801-4-0 (e)

Contents

Endorsements

"I have interviewed, coached and trained thousands of people in the past 25 years and very few have stood out like J. Ibeh Agbanyim. His expertise in the field of human behavior, success psychology and inspirational motivation is outstanding. As well as his command of language! In this modern world of "distractions," "quick fixes" and "ignorance," he eloquently shows you how to improve your life by applying positive psychology and desire thinking. It was such an honor to have worked with Ibeh and a team co-authoring an Amazon International Bestseller. As a neuroscientist specialized in unblocking psychosomatic illnesses through activating human potential, I recognize powerful change makers when I see them. Ibeh is one of these! I highly recommend his latest book THINK which will give you thought-provoking and practical strategies to lead a more fulfilling life."

—Diana Dentinger, **Bestselling Author, Modus Vivendi-Your Life Your Way; International Speaker & Trainer; Creator of The Change Your Game Formula™, Founder of The Meaning of Life School; Owner of the Life & Leadership Academy™, Creator of the Personality & Needs Profile™, Italy, Europe, www.dianadentinger.com**

"Think is a compelling journey of self-discovery. It takes readers into a new level of cognitive exploration that is guaranteed to produce positive results for anyone up for the challenge. It is perfect to use as a bibliotherapy tool for guiding clients to a realm of insight that cannot be fully accomplished during typical therapy sessions. The engaging style of writing backed with cutting edge research makes this book an exciting and rewarding read for anyone ready to be a successful thinker."

—Dr. Rashida A. Jones, **Psy.D, Licensed Clinical Psychologist, Behavioral Health Practitioner, Founder of Catalyst Consulting Associates, LLC, VA, USA**

"We have the capacity to think and evaluate what course of action we'll take. As J. Ibeh Agbanyim and Raveen Arora discuss in the book, THINK, critical thinking is vital and could help prevent adverse decisions and awful consequences in life. What would Adam and Eve's life be like had they not eaten the apple and more carefully considered God's warning? Perhaps they should have evaluated their options and consequences, in advance. Perhaps family problems and even wars can be prevented when we employ critical thinking skills. The book, THINK, while a major contribution to Psychology and in particular, Cognitive Psychology, should be read by everyone who wants to use critical thinking processes and prevent adverse reactions in their lives. I highly recommend J. Ibeh Agbanyim and Raveen Arora's book to all."

— *Sam Sterk*, **Ph.D., CC-AASP # 177, Sport Psychologist and Hypnotherapist; Author of Win! Get the Mental Edge Skills in Martial Arts, and**

J. Ibeh Agbanyim and Raveen Arora truly awaken the human perception and deliberation about life and our inner construct, when they simply state that, "…thinking is hard work. People will do whatever it takes to avoid thinking." Based upon research undertaken about statistics of inmates in American prisons, this book challenges the reader, particularly critical thinkers and takes them on a journey of new self-discovery that involves every aspect in life. I highly recommend THINK to individuals from all walks of life. This book not only is incredibly thought provoking, but keeps the reader engaged throughout!!

—*Sairah Qureshi*, **PhD, President of Action Against Bullying, LLC, Anti-Bullying Consultant & Specialist, and author of "Bullying and Racist Bullying; What ARE We Missing?" (Eds 1 & 2), New Jersey, USA**

"Think is a thought-provoking piece of work that challenges readers to self-examine and view people as 'souls and not suspects.' When we allow ourselves to see people for who they can become and not who they currently are; humanity will be uplifted."

— *Govind Arora*, **President-Stanley Black & Decker, Latin America Group, Fort Lauderdale, FL**

Humanity transcends geographical location, social status, gender, race, religion, or national origin. It takes discipline of thoughts, self-awareness, and engagement to embrace humanity. This book is a road map to finding oneself in the process.

v

"Although deliberate and strategic thinking is not easy, Think is an easy to read, powerful and inspirational book. The talented authors, J. Ibeh Agbanyim and Raveen Arora, cite specific studies supporting the fear, perceived vulnerability and consequences associated with the avoidance of thinking. The profound concepts on Think are written in a manner that allows the reader to progress effortlessly while traveling on the path toward self-awareness. The book offers a process that enables the reader to take action, in achieving self-discovery. I highly recommend Think to individuals interested in elevating the quality of their life journey while influencing their definition of success."

"Thoughts must go somewhere when new ones come along. But why can I think of something before my neighbor, or vice versa? Somehow deep in the digs of the human brain that God uniquely fashioned is the wiring to allow the wondrous thing called thought to roil into expression. It may take another step to transform to language. Once we recognize our singularity, our oneness, we embrace the immeasurable fortune that those thoughts guide us through the daunting forest of life inside unique bodies distributed randomly across the planet, often our peril."

—Lawn Griffiths, Former Religion Editor, Tribune
Newspapers

Foreword

Few would argue the fact that we live in an incredibly fast-paced, sound bite world—a world described thusly by early nineteenth-century poet William Wordsworth: "The world that is too much with us; late and soon, Getting and spending, we lay waste our powers; Little we see in Nature that is ours; We have given our hearts away, a sordid boon!" For many, though clearly not for all, information is available at our fingertips within seconds. Our communications can connect us with those in other parts of the world with minimal interruption and effort. Yet so many of us are hypnotized by the reality of the fast and the effortless, the sense that the world requires our sprinting along in the name of innovation and progress.

The authors of Think: The Foundation of Self-Awareness and Engagement, Raveen Arora and J. Ibeh Agbanyim, challenge the myth that humans are islands, futilely striving and thriving in isolation from one another. They posit that because all humans are connected and interconnected sometimes in profoundly simple and sometimes in complex ways that our efforts to coexist often give rise to the worst that is our humanity. These demonstrations of failures to connect and failures to understand bombard us all via news stories and headlines, too often showcasing the worst that is our humanity. To divide and conquer and to value competition over collaboration is to leave us all with something potentially missing. To think about losses in the face of gains is to be more reflective and more deliberate in our own efforts to make sense of the world.

In her introduction to her play Fires in the Mirror (1992), actor and playwright Anna Deveare Smith posits that "the mirrors of society do not mirror society." I chose to read Smith's statement as both an observation and a challenge, an observation that what we see in human behaviors and actions may not match the narratives we construct in our heads about any given circumstance or situation. Equally, her sentiment here is a challenge to pause and reflect on the mirrored images we are creating both of ourselves and of those around us for convenience and for safety and security, avoiding the fears that leave us vulnerable and out–of-control. To take risks, to acknowledge our own frailties, mistakes and missteps, according to these authors, is to acknowledge the fullness of our individual and shared humanity.

A number of useful takeaways emerge from this small text. Each reader is asked to think critically about our roles in all of our relationships, both the personal and the professional. We are each invited, albeit challenged in fact to access our humanity quotient through the Arizona State University Project Humanities Humanity 101 principles—respect, integrity, empathy, forgiveness, compassion, kindness, and self-reflection. To practice these values daily is to take a higher road when those around us unknowingly or knowingly take us into their abyss of moral and ethical despair, confusion and chaos. Theirs is not advice that harps on our human frailties and shortcomings but rather advice to empower us to think more about who we are and how we exist and co-exist in the world. Theirs is not a prescription for worldly success and gain via material excess and empty acclaim but rather a bold reminder that we cannot always control what happens in the world but we do have some degree of control over how we react to whatever happens. Thinking makes sense, thinking human does not make us immune to the evils and disappointments of the world. Thinking makes us human and how we treat each other is therefore the measure of our own humanity.

—*Neal A. Lester*, PhD, Foundation Professor of English and Founding Director of Project Humanities, Arizona State University

Dedication

We dedicate these nuggets of wisdom to everyone who hungers for self-efficacy, self-awareness, self-discovery, intellectual humility, and spiritual intelligence. To those with the audacity to advocate for diversity and inclusion—and to those who are eager to make a difference in the world but don't know how or where to start. We dedicate this book to you.

Preface

I have learned that it is difficult if not impossible to rise above the way I think. If I don't expand my horizon by interacting with people from different ethnicities, backgrounds, nationalities, religions, age groups, genders, sexual orientations and so on, I position myself to live a dogmatic life. It is also challenging to rise above the way I think if I don't read. Reading different types of works from scholarly journals, magazines, newspapers, books, etc. has revolutionized the way I think and live my life. I will share a couple of examples of how I have evolved and continue to evolve. I now respond, rather than react, to certain situations. But, I still have long way to go in my journey of translating my thoughts into measurable actions.

Over a decade ago, I had an experience that launched me on this journey of thought transformation. As an African-born immigrant living in America, I am aware of how black men are viewed from other races. And it is a good thing to be brutally honest about race and racism in America, because it is one way of healing ignorance, and at same time being present in time and space. Living in the now and being honest with oneself is a powerful tool to fight biases, untested assumptions, and dogmatism. The worst life to live is a life of denial and self-abandonment. To live a life of denial simply means to pretend that certain situations do not exist. Denial leads one into the feeling of self-abandonment. Self-abandonment is when a person dismisses everything they know to be true and embraces everything that other people project. They live a life of pretense driven by the opinions of others about themselves. —When I embarked on this journey of thought transformation, I realized that "the way I once knew it may not be the only way." So I started challenging my own thinking by examining everything that has a negative connotation and could potentially result in controversy.

"Where are you from?"

On a Saturday morning in Arizona around 3am, I was cruising with a friend in a rented, black, late-model car on I-17, heading south to East Valley where I live. We were playing a CD of African music called Makossa and Soukoss. We became carried away with the rhythm of the instruments and vocalists and forgot to obey the city speed limit. I looked three hundred feet ahead and saw a State Trooper. Needless to say, we were pulled over for speeding. The officer radioed in a back-up officer. When the cop approached our vehicle, he asked us to provide our insurance, car registration, and driver's licenses for identification. As I was providing the documents, the officer asked me, "Do you know why I pulled you over?" I answered. His next question was "Where are you from?" The officer's second question raised a question in my head. Is he asking my nationality or what? Since I was not sure, I paused for a few seconds to make sure that I understood the question. At that point, the officer rephrased the question: "Where are you coming from?" The clarification of his question made a world of difference, and I was able to provide a coherent answer.

The officer's second question could have been interpreted as racist. Since both officers were of a different race than my friend and me, we could have easily inferred that there was some racial bias. But when I thought about it for few seconds (without saying a word), I gave the officer a chance to rephrase the question for clarity. That simple experience got me thinking. I wondered if I would have answered according to my initial understanding, in other words if I would have stated my nationality, if that night could have turned ugly? I then would have ended up accusing the officers of being racists based on my initial, untested assumption and ill-prepared assessment. Such an accusation would have provoked the officers and of course escalated into an ugly situation. I was able to salvage the situation, however, by simply thinking about my own thinking—which meant reexamining my question in my mind before opening my mouth to say the first thing that came into my head. This is an example of how thinking about what to say before saying it can defuse a situation. Thinking first can prevent heartaches, divorces, job loss, racial tension, and other negative outcomes befalling humanity. Think of a situation in your experience where you spoke too soon and created a damaging episode. Consider how you could have avoided that outcome by simply pausing and thinking about what to say before saying it.

Second Example

Often times when I "hang out" with friends, we talk about various topics of interest, from everyday life experience to scholarly or scientific issues. On one occasion, I had a discussion with a group of friends who had backgrounds in psychology, political science, engineering, constitutional law, and social work. The discussion was over which candidate was qualified to become the president of the United States of America. The conversation became heated with personal opinions, sentiments, and emotional attachments over the contesting candidates and not so much about their political achievements or measurable political contributions. At some point I thought to myself, I'm not a political scientist or a politician.

Why am I debating with a constitutional law attorney and a political scientist on a topic that I have limited knowledge about? It dawned on me that I was debating with political experts based on emotions and not facts. The moment I made that declaration in my mind, I was able to listen and learn from individuals who had devoted their lives to study and become experts in their subjects. I wonder how many of us engage in arguments over subjects about which we have no knowledge and therein refuse to pause, think, and allow those who are authorities on the subject to educate us? Thinking about our own thinking before we act is what this book is all about.

This book will present real-life examples of situations that challenge our way of thinking and hopefully will entice readers to pause and think before engaging in situations that could turn ugly. None of us is immune from making hasty decisions, or hasn't engaged in poorly processed information that ended up producing a regrettable experience as a result.

Introduction

A recent study from Harvard University and the University of Virginia concluded that sixty-seven percent of men resent metacognition as opposed to twenty-five percent of women (Wilson, Reinhard, Westgate, Gilbert, Ellerbeck, Hahn, Brown, & Shaked, 2014). This research is an indication that, in essence, thinking is hard work. People will do whatever it takes to avoid thinking. Finding something to do that requires minimal thinking is less work, particularly for men. Men would rather engage in something outside of their own thoughts than to sit down and ponder a problem, and this can be a dangerous prospect in certain arenas where they have responsibilities involving the welfare of others. To confront their own thoughts is frightening and revealing. When I read this study, the first question that came to mind was, is it possible that men get in more trouble than women because they refuse to get in touch with their thoughts? In America, more men are incarcerated than women. And, incarceration is a result of poor judgment and decision-making. Poor judgment could be an indication of a lack of critical thinking skills. The purpose of this book is to invite readers to look inside themselves—to examine the familiar and venture into the unfamiliar for the purpose of self-discovery. The study above is a reminder of what is essential in life: "knowing thyself." Self-awareness is a critical component of living a fulfilled life. It is also foundational. Self-awareness is fundamental because it exposes us to who we really are, what makes us tick, or what gets us excited. In order to get to a place of relevance, thinking is required. We are seeking a new beginning, and that new beginning requires cognitive participation and physical engagement. In other words, action is the interpreter of thoughts. The only way to measure what a person is thinking is by watching what a person is doing. Therefore, there is a correlation between what we think and what we do.

As we journey through this book, we ought to make mental notes of how to improve our thought processes and how to translate what we have learned into actions. We also ought to take notes so that we can revisit what we have learned. Studies show that taking physical notes helps brain activity and retention. Take advantage of this information and document lessons derived from this book, in order to be critical, creative participators in healthy living.

Note

Wison, T. D., Reinhard, D. A., Westgate, C. E., Gilbert, D. T., Ellerbeck, N., Hahn, C., Brown, C. L., and Shaked, A. (2014). *People Would Rather Experience An Electric Shock Than Be Alone With Their Thoughts.* Retrieved from, http://www.iflscience.com/brain/people-would-rather-experience-electric-shock-be-alone-their-thoughts#ZOUd40Wo3aukYcYG.99

Acknowledgments

We wrote this book standing on the shoulders of pioneers who have written materials on THINK. We made conscious efforts to add new stories to old, familiar, day-to-day life experiences. This book celebrates the work of humanitarians across the globe who have made significant contributions in social and cultural advancement. Special recognition goes to Jim Stovall, founder of Narrative Television Network (NTN), whose body of work has helped millions to live fulfilled lives. To Frank Shankwitz, co-founder of Make-A-Wish-Foundation, who has helped bring joy to over 300,000 terminally ill-children. And to all who dare to carry on in the traditions of Mother Teresa, Dalai Lama, and Dr. Neal Lester with Arizona State University Project Humanities. This book shares perspectives of everyday experience from all walks of life.

Special thanks to our team who made this work a reality— our publisher, John Westley Clayton; our editor, Krista Hill. We appreciate your professionalism and vigor.

Chapter 1

Why Think?

We cannot solve our problems with the
same thinking we used when we created
them.

—Albert Einstein

Thinking brings imagination or ideas into an examination room. In other words, thinking brings imagination to trial—a trial that examines every aspect of a thought. It is through thinking and application that ideas come into existence. Nothing ever existed without going through thought processes. If we look around us, everything ever created came into existence through the power of applied thoughts. For example, before a person chooses what school to attend, where to live, whom to marry, he or she must first think about it. A graduate looking for a job first of all determines which companies to apply to based on location, salary scale, etc., Even after all these needs are met, other thought processes present themselves. Upon being hired into a new job, decisions must be made on how to adapt to the organizational structure. After observing and adapting into the new culture, thoughts of increasing performance and maintaining healthy business relationships

1

become an ongoing exercise. If we look at this construct called thought, it is an ongoing process. It never ends. Even while we are asleep, the mind is still processing information. This is why, upon waking, we are able to remember nearly everything that happened in our dreams. Our minds are constantly processing information.

There is no way an average human being can stop processing information. Even under sedation, the mind still continues to record information. It is the powerhouse that determines our quality of life. Thinking is the cornerstone of human existence. It is in our best interest to examine this construct in terms of measuring how we think, what we want to think about, and when to shift gears in our thinking. To begin, we should first of all understand the importance of thought and how it applies in our daily activities.

The Importance of Thinking

Psychologist Scott Geller from Virginia Tech University explains that thinking is self-talk or internal verbal behavior. He suggests that it is safe and healthy to internally verbalize. For example, when a driver is buckling up for safety, self-talk acknowledges the behavior. In this context, while putting on a seat belt, it is important to have internal verbal behavior on the benefits of wearing a seatbelt. By verbalizing the process, it helps actualize the practice of safety. By considering the exercise the person is present or mindful of the act. Drawing from Dr. Geller's example, thinking about what one is doing creates the sense of being present. Internal verbal behavior or self-talk engages the person in the activity at hand.

Being mindful of what one is doing it reduces human error. Engaging in self-talk enables the adjustment of behavior per situational factors. This simple but critical exercise literally saves lives on a daily basis and applies in every situation because it creates the sense of presence. Being present in our thoughts brings our whole being into oneness and unison. In other words, we are telling ourselves, "We are here at this particular moment in time doing X." Whatever one is doing at that particular moment is what matters. For this exercise to be real and functional, thinking is required.

To test your level of presence at this particular moment, ask yourself, what are you doing right now? Verbalize what it is that you are doing. For example, "I am reading a paragraph about _____." By engaging in self-talk or internal verbal behavior you bring your universe into your conversation and action. Self-talk reduces worry, anxiety, procrastination, and other negative behaviors that happen when our minds wander off. Thinking about what one is doing at a particular moment helps the body calm down. The important thing to remember in this exercise is to give reasons for whatever one is doing, and to be aware whether you are other-directed or self-directed. The point is not to choose an either/or response. One can be motivated by both external and internal controls (Scott Geller, 2005). The point is to be self-aware and engaged.

A recent study from Georgia State University and published in the Journal of Consulting and Clinical Psychology demonstrates that self-awareness reduces aggression, especially toward women. In the study, men who were intoxicated participated in intervention manipulation and demonstrated less alcohol-related physical aggression toward women. This is an indication that self-awareness requires presence and thinking. For example, if a person understands the consequences of demonstrating an inappropriate behavior toward another person and thinks through such behavior, they are more likely to behave with civility. Creative or critical thinking not only encourages self-talk or internal verbal behavior, it also shows in a person's mannerisms. Thinking about our own thinking produces socially positive results.

Thinking About our Own Thinking

Thinking about our own thinking is comprised of two components: regulation of cognition, and knowledge of cognition. Scientists call the process of thinking about our own thinking meta-cognition behavior. A study by Chwee Beng Lee, Noi Keng Koh, Xin Le Cai, and Choon Lang Quek (2012) highlights the role parents play in assisting children's monetary decision-making processes. In other words, thinking about our own thinking is a learned behavior. It is an exercise that improves over time if one continues to engage in self-talk or internal verbal behavior. In terms of training children on how to make monetary decisions, it is critical that parents explain the process in the least complex fashion and reward good behavior when achieved. By so doing, children learn how to think about their own thinking. Also, children learn how to maneuver their thinking in the direction of healthy applications. By practicing metacognition, children understand what thinking is all about.

The same principles apply to adults. Repetition of behavior builds character and perpetuates thinking generations. It is important to understand that revisiting our thought processes before acting is a healthy practice. Acting on our first instincts could give negative results as it could be based on a distorted view. In other words, acting on the first thought that comes to mind might be compromised by emotions. And when emotions cloud logic, in most cases it turns out to be the less preferable approach (except perhaps in emergency situations). To be safe in our thinking journey, rethinking what it is that we are thinking helps us come to the most productive and efficient decisions. The concept of thinking about our own thinking is chronicled in a book entitled You Are the Placebo, by Dr. Joe Dispenza (2014). Dispenza concludes that people can heal themselves with thoughts alone, without using any prescription drugs. Although this method requires mind-training and specific steps, it is possible. Conversely, people can think themselves into sickness and misfortune. We become what we think on a daily basis. Imagine how many times we think ourselves into success or failure? There is power in what we think about. It is critical that we guard our thoughts, because they become our realities.

One might ask, "How do we learn to think?" This is a valid question because human beings are creatures of habit. Early life experiences precondition us to automatic or default responses. There are different types of thinking. We might not cover all of them, but we can share at least four different types to give readers an idea of the different modes of thought.

Four Types of Thinking

Creative and critical thinking go hand-in-hand. Researchers Richard Paul and Linda Elder in 2014 explained creative thinking as how we learn new concepts in making sense of our experience. In comprehending a new subject field or language, in reading, writing, speaking, and in listening, our minds engage in full-fledged creative acts. In other words, when we run into a new experience, our minds try to capture the essence of the experience and what lesson we are to learn from such experience. Creative thinking is what helps us cope within our environment. Creative thinking is foundational and fundamental in nature. It is what helps us organize, shape, interpret and make sense of the world. One example that comes to mind is a new parent learning how to use a baby car seat. New parents will engage in understanding and interpreting information or training on how to use a baby car seat. In the process of learning how to use a baby car seat, creative thinking is applied. Critical thinking is what further analyzes the experience.

Critical thinking assesses and judges information. In other words, after the creative thinking has organized, interpreted and made sense of an experience, critical thinking analyzes and judges the experience. This means both creative and critical thinking work hand-in-hand for a complete, total experience. Using the example of a new parent, after learning how to use the baby car seat, the critical thinking parent would want to know how long the car seat will last. Is it worth the money spent? What is the safety rating, portability, etc? It is important to understand the differences among thought processes so that we can educate ourselves and work well in teams, which is the third type of thinking to be discussed in this chapter: design thinking.

Design thinking is discussed by Tim Brown, CEO and president of the innovation and design firm IDEO. Design thinking is an approach that encourages individuals from different fields of training to come up with ideas to simplify particular processes for the greater good. Using the car seat example, the design-thinking person might suggest that a car manufacturing company work with the car seat company; various safety personnel could come together to determine how all agencies would ensure the safety of the product. . Instead of the three agencies working independently, they now come together for their common purpose. Linda Naiman, founder of Creativity at Work, says that a design mindset is not problem-focused; it is solution-focused and action- oriented towards creating a preferred future. In this instance, a design thinker encourages collaborative exercise to promote a common purpose in the most efficient way. From a psychological approach, a solution-focused and action-oriented attitude encourages positive affirmation, which in psychology is known as "desire-thinking."

Researchers Gabriele Caselli, Mara Soliani, and Marcantonio Spada in a 2013 study defined desire-thinking as a voluntary cognitive process involving verbal and imaginal elaboration of a desired target. This means that an individual will think of what he or she desires and talks about it in a positive light. Affirming one's desire creates optimism, which eventually can lead to action and achievement. Viewing thinking from this multi-faceted approach helps readers to understand the importance of thinking in our lives and also engages readers to be self-aware in their day-to-day endeavors. It is up to us to understand different types of thinking and how to apply them to our individual advantage.

Takeaways from this Chapter:

- Thinking is a critical component in human existence.
- To be an effective thinker, it is important to engage in self-talk and internal verbal behavior.
- Thinking about our own thinking reduces human errors and can be used to teach children monetary decision-making.
- There are different types of thinking, but only four are discussed in this chapter: creative, critical, design, and desire thinking.

The next chapter is entitled Think Human. The idea behind the title was introduced by a Humanitarian and Diversity Awards recipient, Raveen Arora. Raveen Arora understands the importance of treating others with dignity, compassion, respect, and integrity. This belief has helped him serve his customers and neighbors within the India Plaza establishment and The Dhaba restaurant since 2003. Since he first opened his Plaza for business, he has had no criminal incidents. This can be due, possibly, to his core principle of "treating people the way we want to be treated." In chapter two, we will share some of the fundamentals of this approach and the science behind humanitarian work, diversity and inclusion.

Notes

Brown, T. (2008). *Design Thinking*,
https://hbr.org/2008/06/design-thinking

Caselli, G., Soliani, M., & Spada, M. M. (2013). *The effect of desire thinking on craving: An experimental investigation.* Psychology of Addictive Behaviors, 27(1), 301-306. doi:http://dx.doi.org/10.1037/a0027981

Gallagher, K. E., & Parrott, D. J. (2016). A self-awareness intervention manipulation for heavy-drinking Men's alcohol-related aggression toward women. Journal of Consulting and Clinical Psychology,doi:http://dx.doi.org/10.1037/ccp0000118

Geller, S. (2005). What's on your mind? thinking is critical to people-based safety(TM). ISHN,39(9),21-21,23.Retrievedfrom http://search.proquest.com/docview/196525310?accountid=35812

Koyle, B. (2014). *The Abundance Project*, http://www.theabundanceproject.com/2014/09/we-cannot-solve-our-problems-with-the-same-thinking-we-used-when-we-created-them/

Lee, C. B., Koh, N. K., Cai, X. L., & Quek, C. L. (2012). *Children's use of meta-cognition in solving everyday problems: Children's monetary decision-making.* Australian Journal of Education, 56(1), 22-39. Retrieved from http://search.proquest.com/docview/1013717315?accountid=35812

Naiman, L. (2015). *Design Thinking as a Strategy for Innovation: Creativity at Work*,

J. Ibeh Agbanyim

http://www.creativityatwork.com/design-thinking-strategy-for-innovation/

Paul, R., & Elder, L. (2006). *Critical thinking: The nature of critical and creative thought*. Journal of Developmental Education, 30(2), 34-35. Retrieved from http://search.proquest.com/docview/228409035?accountid=35812

Chapter 2

Think Human

Thinking is difficult, that's why most
people judge.

—Carl Jung

Human beings across the globe have fundamental and universal needs to feel relevant. Human beings need shelter, food, a sense of belonging, self-esteem, dignity, compassion, integrity, respect and so forth. When these fundamental factors are disrupted due to one event or another, human dignity is insulted and undermined.

So many great minds walk on this path of "Think Human": Dr. Martin Luther King, Jr., Mahatma Gandhi, Mother Theresa, Former US president Jimmy Carter, Jim Stovall, Frank Shankwitz, Raveen Arora and countless unsung others. These are people who understand the efficacy and potency of treating people the way we want to be treated. Raveen Arora understands the urgency of treating people with dignity, compassion, respect, integrity, and love, irrespective of their backgrounds. He demonstrates these qualities on a daily basis in his India Plaza restaurant along the Apache corridor. Raveen exemplifies what it means to "Think

Human". As an entrepreneur, community cornerstone, philanthropist, author, mentor, and humanitarian, he believes in the following principles:

- Place purpose before profit
- People before process
- Culture before strategy
- Stakeholders before shareholders

During Arora's Economic Driver Award's acceptance speech from the Greater Phoenix Chamber of Commerce Impact Award Luncheon in 2016, he reiterated his core business principles as mentioned above. His business beliefs explain why his establishment is so successful and impactful to the community and humanity at large.

Purpose before Profit

Definite purpose is one of Napoleon Hill's principles that validates his seventeen principles of success. "Whatever the mind can conceive and believe, the mind can achieve." If the mind is clear on what it wants, it shall surely accomplish it. Profit in business is the offspring of definite purpose. In other words, when the mind is focused and determined to achieve a goal, any obstacles in the way must defer to the destiny. Raveen believes that quality service is a priority for business sustainability. He ensures that his products and services are first class. It is when purpose is strategically defined and delivered that profit is realized over time. Purpose without people to help actualize it becomes a mirage.

People before Process

One benefit of having a sense of focus on a worthy goal is the cultivation of healthy relationships. (Hedberg, Brulin, Alex, & Gustafson, 2011). Human relationships are a critical component in business. It is more important than process. Relationships, whether in social settings or the workplace, require the ability to connect with one another. Interestingly, there is no process without people. The moment organizational leaders, decision makers, and employees understand that people come before process, human relationships becomes humane and progressive. Raveen applies this principle with his customers, neighbors, and anyone else he comes in contact with, irrespective of gender, religion, nationality, social status, culture, etc. A recent 2013 study shows "that the overall performance increase was largest when several workers in a group were rewarded, and considerably less when only the best worker in a group, or everyone in the group, got a special mention." Collective and inclusive recognition have more positive influence than individual recognition in the long run, suggesting that group recognition has a more consistent, positive force. Kimberly Merriman, an associate professor of management at the University of Massachusetts, concludes that employees feel disappointed if they expect a reward and do not receive any; therefore, it is perhaps more effective to maintain an element of surprise in acknowledging performance, rather than condition employees to anticipate or expect it.

Culture before Strategy

People create culture over a period of time by living and working within a geographical area. Culture is formed as a result of groups of people coming together for a common purpose. People and culture are what define humanity, because, as John Donne wrote, "no man is an island." Raveen Arora understands the importance of people and when they come together for business and relationships purposes. When people come together for a common objective, culture is formed in order to perpetuate such experience. After culture is formed, the strategies for co-existence are designed.

From a business perspective, organizational culture is formed by individuals who have a stake in the organization. In other words, an organizational culture is established based on mission, vision, purpose statement and strategies. In 2013, researchers Bing Li, Jianpeng Zhang, and Xiaoxia Zhang suggested that organizational culture influences knowledge management practices. Knowledge management encompasses strategic assets and sources of competitive advantage in organizations. People bring their expertise to the company and organizational culture, thereby improving organizational strategy. An organization is as strong as the people who work in the company. Raveen understands the importance of creating a healthy organizational culture for the purposes of well-being, customer satisfaction and community viability.

Stakeholders before Shareholders

Raveen Arora emphasizes taking care of his stakeholders and shareholders for two reasons:

• It is the right thing to do

• It ensures the viability of the employees, the company and the economy

Taking care of stakeholders is an integral part of operating a business. Stakeholders include employees of the company, customers, and anyone who has an interest in the welfare of the company. It is critical to ensure that stakeholders are treated with dignity, respect, compassion, and integrity because of moral obligation. It is not a choice or negotiable. Imagine a family going into a restaurant, and the waitperson acts uncivil and uncooperative. When reported to the manager, nothing is done about it. The family will not likely visit the restaurant again. A leader who does not appreciate customer satisfaction puts his or her business at risk. The right thing to do is to ensure that people are treated the way that any person wants to be treated. Raveen maintains and utilizes this principle and in turn his stakeholders and shareholders feel appreciated.

When customers, neighbors and community are treated humanely, it is difficult for people not to reciprocate. The same principle applies when people are treated with hostility and indifference. It breeds tension, aloofness, unhealthy stresses and other negative energies within work environments and human space in general. If we as people can treat our environment with a sense of belongingness, acceptance, and humility, our communities and societies will mirror what we exhibit to the universe. To put it in a broader perspective, our communities and societies are reflections of how we view one another. Raveen's restaurant and marketplace attracts people from all walks of life—a representation of diversity, inclusion, societal and communal vitality. One true story Raveen presented at the Arizona State University Project Humanities event sums up what it means to "Think Human".

J. Ibeh Agbanyim

Is this You?

It was a memorable experience to have witnessed Raveen's acceptance speech as a Don Carlos Humanitarian Award recipient in 2015. It is an annual event to honor individuals who not only go above and beyond in their efforts to help others with special needs but also contribute to the economic vitality of the city of Tempe. Three months after the event, Raveen was at his marketplace one afternoon when a tall, young man in his twenties, with a chain hanging out of his pocket, walked in looking a bit anxious. Raveen greeted him and asked if he could assist him. The man declined, saying he was ok and continued to browse expensive items on the shelves. Five minutes later, Raveen again offered to assist him and his response was the same: "Thank you. I'm ok." The third time Raveen offered to help, the young man repeated his same response, butt his time he thrust his hand deep in his pocket. Raveen was unsure what he was doing. Finally, the young man pulled out a black object and thrust it in Raveen's face, asking him "Is this you?"

Looking closer, it was a cell phone with a picture of Raveen. Raveen did not know how to respond. The young man told Raveen that he had been in attendance when Raveen received his Humanitarian award and that he attempted to approach him to shake his hand; he was prohibited by security officials. He had been trying to find Raveen ever since. He had walked six miles to meet him. Raveen humanized his experience when he talked about the love he had for his mother. After the young man expressed his deepest emotions to Raveen, they hugged each other. Raveen served him lunch and assisted him financially for that day.

The experience might have been different had Raveen reacted suspiciously or otherwise negatively to the young man.

16

Sometimes, a split-second decision makes a world of a difference in how a situation turns out. In this instance, Raveen said that he responded to the young man with a sense of openness and humanity.

We "think human" when we treat one another with respect and dignity. We "think human" when we place purpose before profit. We "think human"when we place people before process. We "think human" when we place culture before strategy. We "think human" when we place stakeholders before shareholders. We "think human" when we think about each other as a soul and not a suspect. When we look at one another as what we could become and not what we are, the world can be more peaceful and forgiving. The next time we meet a new face, "think human" by seeing them for what they could become and not what we perceive they are.

The next chapter discusses the unconscious biases in all of us. By reading this chapter, we will become aware of unconscious biases and learn how to regulate them. This chapter will also discuss the signs that indicate when we are experiencing or acting on unconscious biases. The whole idea is to create a safe avenue to discuss and be aware of our unconscious biases.

J. Ibeh Agbanyim

Notes

Hedberg, P., Brulin, C., Aléx, L., & Gustafson, Y. (2011). *Purpose in life over a five-year period: A longitudinal study in a very old population.* International Psychogeriatrics,23(5),806-13.doi:http://dx.doi.org/10.1017/S1041610210002279

Li, B., Zhang, J., & Zhang, X. (2013). *Knowledge management and organizational culture: An exploratory study.* Creative and Knowledge Society, 3(1), 65-n/a. doi:http://dx.doi.org/10.2478/v10212-011-0031-3

Schoenberger, C. R. (2016). *The Right—and Wrong—Ways to Give Employees Kudos: A company's productivity can be improved by recognizing some employees' hard work,* http://www.wsj.com/articles/the-rightand-wrongways-to-give-employees-kudos-1464660022

Chapter 3

Unconscious Bias

Be a rainbow in someone else's cloud.
—Dr. Maya Angelou

Unconscious bias has always been a sensitive issue. It fosters negative imagery and impressions, particularly in American society. This chapter is not to address known issues of bias; however, interest is focused on those biases many of us have without being aware. The second purpose of this chapter is not to point fingers or blame one another for whatever insecurities we have, but to discuss cognitive or hidden behaviors that suggest the presence of unconscious biases. Hopefully, by encouraging self-awareness in this discussion, we can start paying attention to those micro-behaviors that speak volumes about our unconscious biases. Reading and understanding this chapter will help us help others.

Biases manifest themselves everywhere, everyday and no one is immune from exhibiting unconscious bias. This is not about being morally superior or righteous; it's about being and acting human. Researcher Narinder Kapur in 2015 emphasized that unconscious bias occurs when such tendencies are outside our awareness and conscious control. Errors can occur that are based on unconscious bias. We all can exhibit unconscious bias, irrespective of academic hierarchy or spiritual well-being. Unconscious bias is a human construct that ought to be dealt with on a conscious and internal level. The moment we make unconscious behaviors conscious, we take ownership of our prejudices and can now control them. Consider this example:

"For example, a patient with a history of heart disease and a recent stent sees a doctor for blank spells, fever, and confusion. The doctor orders an ECG. It's normal, so he orders an echocardiogram, which is also normal. The next day he orders a cardiac angiogram, which is also normal. The next day the patient has a seizure, so the doctor orders a brain scan, which shows high signal abnormality in both temporal lobes, strongly suggestive of limbic encephalitis, which is substantiated by subsequent investigations. The doctor kept looking for evidence to confirm his initial hunch rather than looking for alternative possibilities." (Narinder Kapur, 2015).

Based on this example, the doctor has no intention of committing any kind of conscious medical error against the patient or the medical system; rather, the doctor keeps looking at what is already known as opposed to the new information at hand. The process of focusing on the already established diagnosis without considering new information could be viewed as unconscious bias without the doctor purposefully showing any kind of bias. To bring this experience to a conscious level, the doctor ought to be open-minded and willing to consider the new information at hand, because "the way we once knew it may not be the only way." Be open to look again to the familiar. A second look may present new ways of seeing old problems.

A study conducted at UCLA Emergency Medical Center by researchers Knox H. Todd, Nigel Samaroo, and Jerome R. Hoffman asks a simple question: When a patient comes in an emergency room at UCLA Emergency Medical Center, does the patient's race determine whether the patient receives pain medication or not? Their study reported that twenty-five percent of white patients as opposed to fifty-five percent of Hispanic patients received less pain medication. Dr. Knox H. Todd went to Emory University in Atlanta and repeated the same study, which showed similar results. When emergency room doctors at both facilities were asked why there were such wide disparities, virtually none of them was aware of such deviations in treatment between Hispanic and non-Hispanic patients and African-American and non-African Americans. This indicates the presence of unconscious bias. Preconceived notions about our environment shape our biases, and negative micro-behaviors have ways of presenting themselves and indicating bias, even though we intend no harm.

This unconscious bias phenomenon is human conditioning and has no bounds. This means all races, ethnicities, nationalities, etc, possess unconscious biases, according to Harvard University Sociologist, Dr. David Williams. He further notes that, if someone holds a negative stereotype about a group and meets someone from that group, their first words are important. Their response will be automatic and unconscious, without the awareness that such behavior was applied. To offer another example, consider that a person prefers women who look a particular way or have a certain shape. When a woman does not fit that particular mental image, the person will exhibit body language, eye movements, facial expressions, and vocal tones that suggest unconscious bias. Or, if a woman prefers tall men, she will gravitate toward them subconsciously. Behaviors induced by unconscious biases cross all demographics without exception.

J. Ibeh Agbanyim

When We Know Better, We Do Better

Being aware of our thoughts encourages diversity of thought. In other words, by allowing ourselves to think outside of our repetitive way of thinking, we can consider other ways of thinking. The idea of diversity of thought is a deliberate, open-minded approach based on research. A recent study by researcher Gugu Mtetwa noted that diversity of thought is not what we think but how we think. It is critical for problem solving. It is also critical to understand that we all have biases based on our upbringing, our environment, and our experiences growing up (Gugu Mtetwa, 2016). Being aware of the universality of biases will help us engage in conscious thoughts and behaviors. According to researchers Gregg Steinber and Lori Gano-Overway's (2003), pervasiveness explanatory style suggests that our experiences in life are universal, not specific. This means that human experience of any kind is a human experience. There is no such thing as only one individual going through a particular problem. Understanding each situation from this perspective is likely to reduce biases, whether conscious or unconscious. To be aware is to be present. Knowing that we all have biases in some fashion is to live life in the now, to examine what is happening in the moment and to embrace the experience, thereby reducing unconscious biases. For example, asking ourselves why we respond in a particular way whenever we see two individuals, one who is overweight while the other is thin. Whatever preferences we have between these two individuals, we should ask ourselves why we feel the way we do. Consciously having a self-talk or internal dialogue forces us to face hard questions and seek out answers, bringing us to self-awareness. Another way to keep unconscious bias in check is to pay attention to our microaggressions. Janis Bellack in a 2015 study emphasizes that microaggressions are often the result of unconscious biases that lead to unintended discrimination against or degradation of those who are socially marginalized in a society, whether for skin color, gender, sexual orientation, age, language origin, religion, disability, or any other characteristic. It is also good to note that unconscious biases are more often than not the root contributors to unintentional, insensitive attitudes and behaviors that reflect innate prejudices or biases. Such biases can be for or against, positive or negative, advantaging some and disadvantaging to others, and are held by all of us whether we are aware of them or are willing to admit to having them (Janis Bellack, 2015). It is clear that we are all guilty of unconscious biases. To deny that we are guilty of unconscious biases is to perpetuate the shadows that plague each and every one of us.

A recent edition of the American Psychological Association's publication, Monitor on Psychology, addresses the subject of unconscious biases as 25,000 Syrian refugees are migrating into Canada. At the Public Mental Health Initiative in Manitoba, Canada, psychologist Rehman Abdulrehman, and six guest editors advised professionals and the public to avoid assuming that all trauma experienced by refugees occurred in their home country. Sources of stressors such as racism, discrimination and Islamophobia can depend on their country of origin. As we have indicated, unconscious biases are pandemic. To be mindful of the emotional, psychological, and social damage unconscious biases can cause—in the lives of aggressors and victims alike—is to further minimize the prevalence of unconscious bias.

How Can We Control Our Unconscious Biases?

Unconscious bias does not discriminate. It is a universal and ongoing personal and social ill. All cultures have unconscious bias challenges. Unconscious bias is not limited to a particular race, religious group, social class, profession, political group, gender, sexual orientation, or nationality. Knowing this enables us, as people of good conscience, to educate ourselves and others on how to identify unconscious bias and elevate our treatment of others to a healthier standard. Of course, a common sense approach always helps.

Treat others the way we want to be treated

This is always the best way of fighting biases toward one another. We all have certain innate expectations, either learned from our environment or from family experience. The universal expectation is, generally, that we expect people to treat us with respect, dignity, humanity, compassion, and all other positive energies associated with healthy living. If we expect such treatment from others, we are obligated to treat others the exact same way. Life has a boomerang effect: what we put out is what we get back in return. It may not happen right away, but eventually it can echo back into our lives through other circumstances. Each time we behave in an unwelcoming way to another person, remember that "there is a pay day." The message is simple: Treat others the way we want to be treated.

Change is a personal commitment

Dr. Viktor Frankl declared that "the most basic human motivation is the will to meaning." We have the willpower to become whatever we envision. How long it takes to achieve a particular goal is important, but the process by which the dream is achieved is even more important. Self-actualization requires tenacity, grit, perseverance, focus, and the "will to meaning." Dr. Maya Angelou cited Terrence, (ca 195-159 B.C.), the Roman playwright who was a slave of a senator before he was freed: "I am a human being.

Nothing human can be alien to me." To make such a declaration requires self-efficacy, self-awareness, humility, and all the positive forces that compel a person to achieve greatness. Dr. Martin Luther King Jr. declared, "Even if I knew that tomorrow the world would go to pieces, I would still plant my apple tree." This simply means do what ought to be done, and not what wants to be done. Do it not because it is popular, but because it ought to be done. Personal commitment builds character over time. It is a measure of self-discipline. If we are really committed to fighting our biases, whether conscious, unconscious, implicit, or unthinking, it requires personal commitment, not group or societal exercise. It starts, rather, with one person's commitment to changing his or her mind about a particular situation. Only when our minds are set on a particular event can we seek support to guide us through the process. For example, a student only learns from a professor after signing up for a program and committing to completing the program. Only then can the influence of a coach or teacher become pronounced and helpful.

The journey of putting our biases in check requires personal commitment, self-awareness, grit, and ongoing self-reminder.

Ask Questions

If there is anything to doubt, doubt our own doubts. It is a difficult thing to confront ourselves, especially in difficult situations. Because of the discomfort in asking ourselves tough questions, we do whatever it takes to avoid self-talk or internal verbal behavior. Instead, we engage in other activities such as video games, talking on the phone for hours, and other diversions that distract us. By constantly running from our thoughts, we continue to nurture our already established perceptions about particular events or circumstances. If we can pause and ask ourselves why we feel the way we feel about a particular person, group or situation, we can then start to unfold and peel away layers of biases that we have held onto for so many years. In order to address the universal issue of unconscious biases, we have to admit that we have them, ask ourselves why we have them, and how we came about formulating such prejudices. Confronting these questions takes us to a place of unfamiliarity and discomfort, but if we continue asking these questions, we then start to see old issues in new ways. Asking questions exposes our fears and doubts. Through this exposure we start to look for answers by consulting trusted avenues that can help us see clearly. Asking close friends and trusted family members always helps. Reading literature on a particular topic helps all the more.

Read with a Purpose in Mind

While not everybody likes to read, reading is healthy in so many ways. Researchers Roxanne F. Hudson, Joseph K. Torgesen, Holly B. Lane, and Stephen J. Turner in 2012 emphasized that reading fluency is an important part of reading proficiency and reading a text fluently is critical for comprehending it. Reading is a critical component in a digital age. Reading literature on the topic of unconscious biases and other types of biases will broaden and educate us as to why we do what we do and how to pre-determine our course of action. In other words, "if we know better, we do better." By reading articles from reputable sources on a particular subject we broaden our scope on that topic. The American Psychological Association journal is always a reliable source for information about psychology-related topics such as unconscious biases and other behavioral discussions. Reading reputable journals and other publications on the topics within this book is therefore highly encouraged. One can reach out to libraries for further assistance. The most important thing is to have the desire to learn, and the rest is discovery.

In the attempt to educate ourselves in reducing our unconscious biases, we in turn can educate others. And when others are educated, they will educate in turn. In the process, we become "a rainbow in someone else's cloud," in the words of Dr. Angelou, and the world is a better and healthier place.

The next chapter discusses the need to follow the Cloud (GPS) and not the Crowd (Naysayers). Following the Cloud is represented by instinct, guts, North Star, intuition, consciousness etc. Following the Crowd, on the other hand, depicts doing things because others are doing it, whether right or wrong, moral or immoral. The bottom-line is that adults know between right and wrong. However, some people choose to anesthetize their consciousness and do the wrong thing. When this happens, an evil doer's moral compass or loud speaker within their consciousness is broken. We will explore questions like, "Are we doing things because we want to do them or because society dictates that we do them?" "Do we think things through before doing them, or are we always on autopilot?"

J. Ibeh Agbanyim

Notes

Bellack, J. P. (2015). *Unconscious bias: An obstacle to cultural competence*. Journal of Nursing Education, 54(9), S63-64. doi:http://dx.doi.org/10.3928/01484834-20150814-12

Chamberlin, J. 2016. Monitor on Psychology. "A new online resource for working with Syrian Refugees." A Publication of the American Psychological Association, June, 2016.Vol. 47. no.6, p. 8.

Eloisa, F. F., Khon, M. A., and Neighbor, M. L. (2002). Lack of Association between Patient Ethnicity or Race and Fracture Analgesia, http://onlinelibrary.wiley.com/doi/10.1197/aemj.9.9.910/pdf

Hudson, R. F., Torgesen, J. K., Lane, H. B., & Turner, S. J. (2012). Relations among reading skills and sub-skills and text-level reading proficiency in developing readers. Reading and Writing, 25(2), 483-507. doi:http://dx.doi.org/10.1007/s11145-010-9283-6

Kapur, N. (2015). Unconscious bias harms patients and staff. BMJ : British Medical Journal, 351 doi:http://dx.doi.org/10.1136/bmj.h6347

Knox, H. T., Samaroo, N., and Hoffman, J. R. (1993). Ethnicity at a Risk Factor for Inadequate Emergency Department Analgesia, http://www.wellassembled.com/sites/international-em/UserFiles/File/IAEMC_Lectures/Ethnicity%20as%20a %20Risk%20Factor%20for%20Inadequate%20Analgesia% 20in%20the%20ED-%20TODD.pdf

Mtetwa, G., C.A.(S.A.). (2016). *BIAS AT THE OFFICE AND DIVERSITY OF THOUGHT*. Accountancy SA, , 21.

Retrieved from
http://search.proquest.com/docview/1780968758?accountid
=35812

Steinberg, G., & Gano-Overway, L. (2003). *Developing optimism
skills to help youths overcome adversity.* Journal of
Physical Education, Recreation & Dance, 74(5), 40-44.
Retrieved from
http://search.proquest.com/docview/215767590?accountid=
35812

Williams, D. H. (2013). Video report,
https://www.youtube.com/watch?v=rd-butFSi4Q

Chapter 4

Follow the Cloud, not the Crowd

If you hear a voice within you, say, you
cannot paint, by all means paint, and that
voice will be silenced.

—Vincent van Gogh

The Cloud, in this chapter, represents the North Star, or in other words our gut instincts or internal GPS. The Cloud is our conscience; it is our moral compass. It is our ethical sensor that tells us when we are out of line. Everyone has a cloud that directs our path on a daily basis. We either follow the Cloud or follow the Crowd. We will read more about the Crowd in later part of this chapter. We will discuss one example of a person who followed her Cloud and examine what this signifies. Mother Teresa followed her Cloud by yielding to her calling as a nun and humanitarian. Through her humanitarian work, the world recognized her as a symbol of hope and a beacon of light to the sick, the homeless, along with those rich or poor, young or old. She exemplified what it means to care for one another, irrespective of national origin, culture, faith, economic status, etc. She believed that love has no color, that the soul has no color. We are all children of God. She made a stellar contribution to humanity. Mother Teresa was a human being. She had emotions like all of us. She had wishes like all of us. She cried when she experienced and witnessed human sufferings. The difference between Mother Teresa and every other human being is that she discovered herself, her inner being (Cloud) and lived a full life. She lived a life of impact. The questions is, are we following our God-given consciousness, our North Star, or are we busy chasing the wind by following other people's opinions about ourselves?

The "Crowd" represents those associations that bring distractions, distortions, and derailment into our lives. The moment we ignore our internal North Star, our gut-instincts, consciousness, or evidence-based studies and instead pursue Naysayers, we position ourselves for destruction. Associations with the Crowd have derailed brilliant minds into drug abuse, sex trafficking, prison, and other forms of mediocrity.

One Fatal Turn

A decade ago, a refugee from northern Africa migrated into the United States of America to escape war-torn experiences and possible death. Upon arrival in the States, with the help of charity organizations and other aide, he secured an apartment, a job, a vehicle, enrolled in a school, and was reintroduced into his community. He was excited and overwhelmed by all the good things in his new home. Life was good. Noticing that his friends were going out to party at the clubs every weekend, one day he decided to join them for a night out. He went to a club without wearing appropriate attire that conformed to the club's dress code. The club security officer refused him entrance. Instead of complying with the security officer, he decided to confront the officer. Eventually, he complied and was granted access inside the club. Out of excitement, he had a little too much alcohol that night. Without notifying his friends, he took off in his car and headed home. He was swerving all over the roads and could not concentrate because he was intoxicated. A few minutes after he left the club, he ran into another motorist at full speed and crushed the other vehicle. Tragically, the other motorist was pronounced dead at the scene. He was arrested and charged with a DUI along with vehicular manslaughter. According to state law, he received the maximum sentence of twenty-one years in prison.

Moral of the Story

The refugee ignored the severe penalties and risks associated with drunk driving in his new country. When he went to the club with his friends, he failed to use good judgment and call for a cab or ask for a ride. The resulting tragedy altered his life, and destroyed another's, forever. If he would have followed his Cloud (instinct, guts, etc), he would have prevented destroying his record and committing such a grievous crime of manslaughter.

Who Am I?

The most beautiful gift ever given to a human being is the gift of self-awareness and the "will to meaning." The ability to study ourselves on a deeper level of consciousness is an experience everyone ought to achieve. Time and time again, history has demonstrated that people who pursue self-awareness live full lives—full in terms of self-awareness, peace of mind, humility, spirituality, and love for others. It is one gift no one can achieve for us. The quest for self-awareness is a lifelong journey. There is no such thing as reaching the pinnacle of life. Self-awareness is infinite. It has no beginning or end, because the more we know ourselves, the less we know about ourselves. To come to a place of questioning and humility is to come to a place of knowing and understanding the infinite consciousness of our existence.

Dr. Viktor Frankl, in his book, Man's Search for Meaning, makes a profound claim: "In psychiatry there is a certain condition known as delusion of reprieve. The condemned man, immediately before his execution, gets the illusion that he might be reprieved at the very last minute. We too, clung to shreds of hope and believed to the last moment that it would not be so bad." As we journey through this maze called life, we observe through the lenses of hope, believing that we create our own world in the laboratory of our souls. Only when we view life through the lenses of self-awareness do we experience contentment and wholeness—living life as we see it and not as we once knew it. Social psychologist Amy Cuddy calls it "presence." In her book Presence, Amy Cuddy says that "By accessing our personal power, we can achieve presence, the state in which we stop worrying about the impression we're making on others and instead adjust the impression we've been making on ourselves." Living in the now does not have to be a yoga course, spiritual journey, "inner transformation" or significant exercise; instead, it must be a daily practice in reminding ourselves how important today is. We need to note the significance of the people we meet, the opportunities we encounter, the incidents that we witness, and the surprises that occur. All these experiences make us who we are. Therefore, by being present, we allow ourselves to go through the day without missing a beat. By exercising simple self-awareness, we allow ourselves to enjoy our days in discovering more about our strengths as well as our weaknesses.

"Who am I?" is an honest but complex question we ought to ask ourselves daily. We play different roles. We wear so many hats. We are husbands, wives, brothers, sisters, managers, supervisors, friends, cohorts, etc. In the end, we are human beings having human experiences. The best way to embrace our experience is to be present and self-aware. When we are self-aware, we follow our North Star or Cloud. Everything boils down to self-discovery. If we recognize ourselves as souls having human experiences, we then understand and celebrate one another without judgment based on race, gender, and so forth. . Instead, we come to a realization that whatever hurts us directly, hurts others indirectly. Understanding that we have limited time in this space called life, we should invest our limited willpower wisely.

Willpower is limited

Research psychologists Dr. Roy F. Baumeister and John Tierney noted in their collaborated book Willpower that "most major problems, personal and social, center on failure of self-control: compulsive spending and borrowing, impulsive violence, underachievement in school, procrastination at work, alcohol and drug abuse, unhealthy diet, lack of exercise, chronic anxiety, explosive anger. Poor self-control correlates with just about every kind of individual trauma: losing friends, being fired, getting divorced, winding up in prison." Ignoring our North Star, Cloud, internal verbal behavior, or self-control is a license for disaster in that we can be destined to lives of mediocrity. . Understanding the importance of self-awareness and self-efficacy is the best thing we can do for ourselves. As Charles Darwin noted in his book, The Descent of Man, "The highest possible stage in moral culture is when we recognize that we ought to control our thoughts." There is something beautiful about controlling our thoughts, and by controlling our thoughts, we control ourselves. It is never healthy to do things because others are doing them. In the omnipresence of peer pressure, social pressure, relationship pressure, or religious pressure, it is critical to step back and self-reflect.

In the end, it is all about us living fulfilled and impactful lives. Let us not allow our Crowds to suffocate or affect our judgment because, in the midnight hour, when the curtain is drawn and no one is looking, only then do we realize it is all about us alone facing our deepest fears and questions. To be in touch with oneself is to know what is possible and what is not. Acknowledge one's Cloud and rethink one's Crowd.

The next chapter puts forth the assertion that "thought without action is lethal." It is well to have all these good thoughts in our minds about how we want to make this world a better place. It is wonderful to want to unite people by holding hands and singing Kumbaya. But all these thoughts are useless if we do not translate them into results or actions. Action is the interpreter of our thoughts. Without actions, our thoughts have no measurable value. Thoughts remain transient—they come and go. That is why it is important to seize the moment, either in writing or in audio, as it occurs. That is what writers, authors, and reporters do. This chapter will attempt to focus on how we can observe our own thoughts and actions in order to live a full life. It is when we match our thoughts with deeds that we experience transformation and self-awareness. As we read this chapter, we should ask ourselves "What good thoughts have we not acted upon?" "How can we improve our ability to entertain positive thoughts and discard those that are negative or toxic?" "Who controls our thoughts?" Enjoy this chapter as we meditate on the points shared.

J. Ibeh Agbanyim

Notes

Amy Cuddy. Presence: *Bringing your Boldest Self to your Biggest Challenges*. New York, N.Y. Little, Brown and Company, 2015.

Baumeister, R.F, and Tierney, J. WILLPOWER: *Rediscovering the Greatest Human Strength*. New York, N.Y. Penguin Group, 2011.

Frankl, V. E. *Man's Search for Meaning*. Boston, Mass: Beacon Press, 2006.

Mother Teresa of Calcutta Center: Official site, http://www.motherteresa.org/layout.html

Vehicular Manslaughter in Arizona, http://cantorcriminallawyers.com/vehicular-crimes/vehicular-manslaughter-in-arizona/

Chapter 5

Thought Without Action is Lethal

Whatever the mind can conceive and
believe, the mind can achieve.
—Napoleon Hill

It is impossible to act on all of the 60,000 thoughts an average brain processes on a daily basis. The ability to translate positive thoughts (about twenty percent of our daily thoughts) into action is what distinguishes imagination from applied thoughts (action). Thoughts without action have no substance. It is like starting an engine of a vehicle and leaving it in idle. Until the gear is shifted into drive or reverse mode, the vehicle will not perform (move) according to its intended purpose (travel), thus producing the progress or result. Therefore, thought has no value until translated into action. For example, many of us have thought about publishing a book. Some people even go as far as starting a manuscript, but do not see it through to completion. Until complete action is executed, the thought of publishing a book becomes an illusion. Many people think about going back to school, but until then enroll, graduating from a program becomes a fantasy. Many people want job security; unless conscious decisions are made to establish oneself, through dedicated performance within one particular company or area of expertise, the idea of job security is far-fetched. People in a broken marriage, thinking about how to resurrect their dying relationship, have no chance until practical steps are taken such as seeking counseling. The teenager who is socially awkward will not overcome his/her insecurities unless they interact with their peers on a regular basis. . Essentially, action is the interpreter of thoughts. Self-awareness and engagement can never be fully realized without outward expression. It is critical to understand that action is the only measure of thought.

An unexpressed thought can be unhealthy, especially if it is negative. In other words, unexpressed thoughts can become toxic to our bodies. We implode when we harbor unhealthy thoughts and grudges. Imploding in this context means having an unhealthy internal conversation without allowing such thoughts to express themselves or vent in a constructive manner. Verbalized thoughts without action can be considered procrastination. And procrastination in some cases can result in disappointment. It is one thing to verbalize a thought, and another thing to support verbalized thought with action. Let's use an illustration to humanize thought and action.

Had I known

Dr. J. is a phenomenal orthopedic surgeon. He is well known in his field. His credentials are impeccable. He possesses numerous awards for excellence and volunteer contributions. Dr. J. has been president of his medical association and a mentor to many medical students. His human, relatable style of teaching is why his students casually refer to him as "Dr. J." He is personable and approachable. Dr. J. is a family man with three grown sons and a daughter. He put his children through medical, law, and engineering schools. Due to his busy schedule and publishing numerous publications, he has no time to travel as he wishes. He promises his wife of thirty-seven years, Jane, that upon his retirement, still a year in the future, they will purchase a luxurious mobile home and travel across North America. While planning his retirement, Dr. J. still loves to volunteer his time and money in shipping wheelchairs to people in developing countries. He genuinely loves assisting people who need his services as a surgeon and a philanthropist. He shares his aspirations with his wife Jane as they lie in bed one evening. They reminisce how God has blessed them with wonderful children and a life together. The doctor per usual kisses his wife a goodnight and they go to sleep. Tragically, Jane dies in her sleep. When Dr. J reaches out to whisper good morning to his sweetheart, he is met with an irresponsive and lifeless body. Dr. J.'s world comes to a complete stop. First, he goes into denial and blames himself as a trained physician for not noticing any signs that his wife may have been ill. Second, he feels he has failed Jane in not fulfilling his promise of taking her for a cross-country trip upon retirement.

What do we make of Dr. J's experience? Remember, there is no right or wrong answer in this case; however, knowing what we know now about Dr. J's workaholic nature and lack of devotion to personal time, what can be derived in terms of thoughts without actions? Moral of the story, we should not hold our lives hostage until we fulfill other obligations. As we think of those things that bring joy and peace of mind into our spirits and souls, let us pursue them with vigor and grace, because our time in this life is short and unpredictable. Life is like dew or mist that evaporates at some point into thin air, never to return. We should seize the moment and live it with passion and enthusiasm. The only thoughts that count are the ones lived out. Every product ever produced came into existence through the power of applied thoughts. Without application, thoughts become an illusion. Using Dr. J.'s example, what can we learn from his experience?

Start small and grow from it

Most establishments start small and grow big. An oak starts as an acorn and over time becomes a tree. To do well in life, we ought to start small and work our way up to larger results. For example, instead of waiting to retire before he traveled extensively, Dr. J. might have taken shorter excursions with his wife from time to time while he was working. We can apply this concept to many areas. If we want to help the needy, we can start with people we know (family members, friends, neighbors, etc). By so doing, we gain confidence and momentum that enable us to reach out and help the larger spectrum, i.e. community, state, nation, and so on. We have heard the adage "Rome was not built in a day." Whatever we think about doing, we can do it in increments by translating our thoughts into focused or collaborated actions. It is very easy to become discouraged when we start with a big dream without having strategic plans. Therefore, to avoid being overwhelmed, start small but stay focused and clear on what it is the next or ultimate goal.

Stay on Track

In his book Focus, psychologist and former science journalist Dr. Daniel Goleman states that attention is like a muscle: if we don't use it right, it can wither, but if we work it right, it will grow. It simply means to exercise our thoughts with defined purpose and to "zoom in" on what it is we want to achieve. The key is to start small and stay focused. It is difficult to make history without focus. Focus is our road map whereby we reach our desired destination. It is important that life's everyday distractions do not divert our attention from our intended goal. Referring to Dr. J.'s example, he did well in focusing on the big picture, which was to help people live a better life; but his other, more personal goal to travel across country was put on hold (procrastinated) because of busy schedules. Unfortunately, his dream of traveling with his wife was brought to a halt by her sudden death. What is that one thing that we have always wanted to do but have not done it due to our hectic schedules? We risk never doing these things by not following up our thoughts with actions. Stay on the track by meeting thoughts with actions, especially those thoughts that translate into positive results and improving humanity at large.

Live well

Health is wealth. Without good health, every other life pursuit becomes hindered or halts completely. Healthy mental habits are critical and start with desired thinking, positive psychology and gratitude. In the final analysis, our lives are measured by how well we live, what contributions we make, and what legacy we leave behind. All the accolades behind our names do not necessarily show how well we live; but, the kinds of relationships we have with people speak volumes about our approach to life. The love we have in our hearts and show to strangers on the streets speaks for us. Although Dr. J. never fulfilled his dream with his wife, his contributions in helping people across the globe speak about his character and aspirations. One critical contribution that could have benefited himself and those close to him never came to pass, because of hesitation and failure to act on his thoughts. To highlight the points in this subparagraph:

What is that one thing we really want to accomplish but keep procrastinating and postponing?

Who is that one person we want to make peace with but never do?

Who is that one person we want to thank for all the hard work and support he/she has given us?

It is never too late to live out our dreams by translating our thoughts into action. As we read this chapter, let us remember that life is interrelated. What affects one directly, affects another indirectly. Make a point to do your part and never worry about what people may say or not say. It is important to live outwardly, with action, and not inwardly, with unfulfilled thoughts or ideas. The latter process can foster regret. If an average brain processes about 60,000 thoughts daily, and if every one of us would translate just one percent of those thoughts into small kindnesses toward others, the world would be a better place.

The next chapter addresses the urgency of identifying the enemy within. The enemy within is the most dangerous intruder in our lives. Without the willpower to resist this enemy, our hopes, dreams, and aspirations go down the drain. We will learn to identify our internal foe and how to utilize our self-awareness and engagement through applying positive psychology, desired thinking, and conscious actions.

Notes

Dvorsky, G (2012). *Sentient Development: "Managing Your 50,000 Daily Thoughts."* Retrieved, June 22, 2014, from, http://www.sentientdevelopments.com/2007/03/managing-your-50000-daily-thoughts.html

Goleman, D. *Focus: The Hidden Driver of Excellence.* New York, N.Y; HarperCollins, 2013.

Hill, N. Founder of *The Science of Success,* from, http://napoleonhill.wwwhubs.com/

Chapter 6

The Enemy Within

The enemy within us is that which deprives us of the ability to achieve self-realization. The enemy within is represented by us lying to ourselves. The enemy within tells us "it is not possible." The enemy within blames other people for our inadequacies. The enemy within is us, parading about in self-pity. The enemy within is us, telling ourselves that we are the only people, group, nationality, faith, sexual orientation who experiences unfair or unjust treatment. The enemy within is us, formulating hypotheses that are not tested or measured. The enemy within is us, running away from facing our true selves. The enemy within is us avoiding the truth.

Can we relate to the story below? Before we are quick to take a position, let us look again at an old story, with a new perspective.

"You are not my Daddy"

In a powerful book written by Thich Nhat Hanh, True Love, a young husband returns from service to realize that his two-year-old-son does not recognize him as his father. His wife had been pregnant at the time he went away to fight for his country. One day, while his wife is out, the young husband tries to convince his son that he is his father. The son replies, "Mister, you're not my daddy. My daddy is somebody else. He visits us every night, and very often she cries with him. And every time my mommy sits down, he sits down too. Every time she lies down, he lies down too." After the young father hears this story from his son, he is saddened and concludes that his wife has been cheating on him. He starts drinking and staying out late every night at the bar. Eventually, the wife becomes depressed by the lack of attention from her husband. After she endures this abuse for some time, she resorts to suicide by drowning herself in a river. When her husband hears this, he is devastated. That night, he lights a lamp and suddenly, the child cries out. "Mister, Mister, it's my daddy, he's come back!" The boy points to the shadow of his father on the wall. "You know, Mister, my father comes every night. Mommy talks to him and sometimes she cries; and every time she sits down, my daddy sits down too." The child had been referring his mother's shadow. The young husband realizes that his wife was not cheating on him.

This story is a clear example of misperception. The young husband fails to ask his wife who is the person that "visits" her at night. His inability to communicate his concerns to his wife disrupted and devastated the relationship to the point of her taking her own life. The young husband is his own enemy by making assumptions and creating a story that is simply not true. One could posit that the wife succumbed to her own internal enemy by not asking her husband about his sudden change in attitude. In the end, they both were victims of their internal enemies.

J. Ibeh Agbanyim

Unintended Consequences

Life has so many twists, turns, and consequences. According to researcher Steven M. Gillon, the law of unintended consequences states that we cannot always predict the results of purposeful action. Based on the previous story, the young husband purposefully chooses to use lack of communication and silence, fomented by alcohol abuse, as a means to torture his wife. Unfortunately, his behavior has an extreme effect on his wife. Subjectively, he could never know that his actions could result in her committing suicide. In this context, his irrational and inhumane behavior has an extreme impact on the situation. It is important that we are aware of possible, unintended consequences in life. Our personal method of addressing issues could have an adverse effect on parties involved. The young husband never thought that his silent treatment toward his wife could have resulted in rendering his son motherless. The ripple effect that follows our behavior can be enormous and detrimental to our relationships. There can be both legal and lethal consequences. The enemy within ought to be held in check at all times. If the soldier would have thought through his actions and communicated his concerns the experience would have been different. Before we make drastic decisions based on assumptions, let us rethink the consequences and possible, unintended consequences as well.

Fighting our Own Shadows

Psychologist Carl Jung first coined the term "shadow aspect" to describe the hidden part of our unconscious that can have negative influence over our behavior. Our shadows feed us with negative feelings about ourselves: our defeatist attitudes, weaknesses, ugly natures, selfishness, and ego driven self (New-Walker, 2010).

When we experience these episodes, we tend to anesthetize our shadows by acting out against the very thing we are fighting against. Many powerful individuals in the world have demonstrated the danger of hiding our shadows by acting against conscience. Let's share one well-documented example of shadow in display.

A powerful governor of a state takes steps to eradicate prostitution in his area. The governor is passionate in his mission and aggressive in his methods to stop the perpetrators. His moves gain national attention and he is held up as an example of effective leadership. However, the governor is eventually caught soliciting prostitutes himself. The Federal Government wiretapped his phone to discover that he was paying thousands of dollars for escort services. His career is ruined and he faces severe consequences. He is forced to admit to his indiscretions and accept his punishment. Based on shadow aspect theory, the governor was actually fighting his own internal enemy (his love for prostitutes); in retrospect, he started outwardly demonizing escorts and denying his inner demon, in this case an attraction to them. Before we are quick to judge the governor, can we ask ourselves what are the shadows that we are fighting against every day in our lives? We need to identify our shadows that affect our behavior in negative ways. If we can identify this enemy within and address it with honesty and authenticity, fulfillment of our dreams and aspirations is possible. Let us use a simple approach to answering our own questions. Hopefully, we come to this approach with consistency and an open mind.

Three Steps to Facing Our Shadows

These three simple steps are proposed to direct us to the solutions. They are not steps to an ultimate solution, but are intended, rather, to create self-awareness and engagement in order to pursue greater goals.

Admit there is a Concern

From a humanistic approach, admitting there is a concern is the first step to finding a solution. Self-examination is a humbling approach to resolving a concern. In the case of the governor, he admitted his wrongdoing. Admitting wrongdoing is us accepting the fact that we do not know it all. It is us humbling ourselves to our weaknesses. It is us positioning ourselves for a change. Please understand that the concern might not be as profound as the governor's, but enough to disrupt our pattern. It is wise to admit to an observation about ourselves when someone makes it. After acknowledging our flaws or admitting our faults, we can ask the critical question "Now what?" It is a question that calls for action. "Now what?" suggests that there is a concern and that we are willing to take necessary measures to correct it. Correcting concerns requires soul-searching, self-efficacy, self-awareness and spiritual intelligence.

Spiritual Intelligence

Researchers Manaswini Dash and Puspita Patnaik in 2015 emphasized that persons who are high in spiritual intelligence are emotionally more intelligent and have better mental health than those with low spiritual intelligence. Results are discussed in the context of Indian values. Drawing from this study, spiritual intelligence is all about having a relationship with power higher than self, or communicating on a frequency higher than self. It is also reasonable to understand that, whenever we discuss the concepts of internal verbal behavior or dialogue, we are referring to getting in touch with self on a deeper level—and facing our shadows in this unconscious arena means being true to self and avoiding denial. Once truth is exposed there is nothing else to say or hide because truth has a touch of finality and a measure of authority. Spiritual intelligence has everything to do with spiritual resources. These resources are rooted in "the ability to find meaning, purpose, and values in our life, connecting our actions and lives to a wider, richer, meaning-giving context." Connecting to self through spiritual intelligence enables us to entertain our shadows and discuss them in a positive light; we can then be free from their influence or turn them into positive forces for good. The longer we harbor shadows, the more toxic they become to our existence. It is healthier to embrace our shadows, entertain them, and share them in a safe and open environment. As anything else, developing our spiritual intelligence might require individuals who have received training in the field.

Seek Professional Help

Because of the complexities in human life, uncovering our own unconscious enemies or shadows might be a challenge. It is highly encouraged to seek professional help in this area of struggle. For example, those with relationship challenges are advised to seek therapy from experts in various forms of family counseling. Those challenged by varying degrees of mental illness should refer to psychiatrists or psychologists. While seeking behavioral assistance of any sort, it is appropriate to share our shadows with experts on emotions, and also appropriate for experts to share emotions as well. Recent study shows that seventy-two percent of psychologists and trainees have cried at some point with patients, with thirty percent having shed tears in the previous four weeks. There is absolutely no shame in seeking professional help from someone who can help patients identify challenges and then advise them on necessary measures to get better. The idea is to gain understanding that it is critical in seeking appropriate help. Getting help encourages us to uncover the enemy within. Take advantages of experts who are available to help within the boundaries of their training.

When it comes to thinking and acting in a healthy and productive manner, we can be our biggest enemies. It is critical to acknowledge that failure occurs because we give permission for it to happen; success, in turn, happens in our lives because we permit such to take place. It is also important to know that if we do not face our shadows, they will one day expose us. We must take the necessary measures to face our shadows. The three steps mentioned are: admit there is a concern; seek spiritual intelligence; consult professional help as needed.

The next chapter discusses living in the now. It starts with the question "What would you tell the world if you had sixty seconds to live? We will address this thought-provoking question together, with the idea of looking at old information with a new approach.

Notes

Collier, L. (2016). GradPsych, *"Navigating the power differential: Is it OK to cry, Patients aren't the only ones to tear up during therapy—sometimes therapists do, too."* The magazine of the American Psychological Association of graduate students, January 2016. Vol. 14, no. 1, p. 38-40.

Dash, M., & Patnaik, P. (2015). Role of spiritual intelligence in emotional intelligence and mental health. Indian Journal of Positive Psychology, 6(3), 279-282. Retrieved from http://search.proquest.com/docview/1759300236?accountid =35812

Gillon, S. M. (2001). *Unintended consequences why our plans don't go according to plan].* The Futurist, 35(2), 49-55. Retrieved from http://search.proquest.com/docview/218566253?accountid= 35812

Hanh, T. N. (2004). *True Love: A Practice for Awakening the Heart.* Escondido, CA: Shambhala Publications, INC, p. 25-31.

New-Walker, A. (2010). *The shadow effect: Illuminating the hidden power of your true self.* Fellowship, 76(7-9), 35. Retrieved from http://search.proquest.com/docview/815407646?accountid= 35812

Chapter 7

What Would You Tell the World if You Had Sixty Seconds to Live?

> Even if I knew that tomorrow the world
> would go to pieces, I would still plant my
> apple tree.
> —Martin Luther

People vs. the State of Illusion remains one of the best docudramas of our time. A group of experts comes together and discusses perception from a psychological perspective, as well as from that of neuroscience, spirituality, metaphysics, quantum physics, and other concentrations. In this docudrama, there is a segment where the thought provoking question, "What would you do if you had sixty seconds to live?" is asked. It is a powerful question that brings attention to what matters right now. It is a question that gives us pause. It is a question that exposes our current mindset. Most importantly, it is a question that will make us think. This question exposes a whole new way of perceiving life because it takes one to a place of foreseeing the future and bringing the future to our doorstep. This question is about us living life the way life ought to be lived. Living in the present and not mortgaging our entire existence until tomorrow (which may never come) is something worth considering.

Let us examine this question using our current state of mind. What goes through our minds when this question is posed? The answer can only come through the state of mind at this particular moment. All the accumulation of experiences—good, bad, and ugly—will roll up into one. The mouth can only speak what the heart feels. In other words, if the mind is weary, tired, overwhelmed, or hopeless, that is exactly what will come out of the mouth. But if the mind is filled with grace, optimism, gratitude, humility, and hopefulness, the mouth will confess as well. This question should not be taken lightly. First, it exposes the present mindset of the person who is answering the question. Second, it calls for a self-inventory. Third, it calls for action. We are going to use an analogy to illustrate this question in an endeavor to humanize this chapter.

"I was not supposed to be here"

A man in his early sixties was asked in the course of a discussion, "what is the biggest failure in your life?" Such a question would likely prompt a person to discuss their life with openness and transparency. But the man's answer was not ordinary or predictable. His answer was, "I was not supposed to be here." His answer was quite confusing. We were not sure whether he understood the question, so the question was repeated to ensure clarity. And his answer was the same: "I was not supposed to be here." When we continued to probe for an explanation, he then explained that during his mother's pregnancy, the doctor had declared him dead in his mother's womb (a stillborn with no heartbeat). During labor, the doctor was preparing to evacuate the stillborn, but somehow, the fetus had a heartbeat. It was a surprise to everybody including the doctor, delivery room nurses, and the pregnant mother. Even after he was born, he still believes, he was not supposed to be here. Fast forward many years after his birth, during his explanation, the sixty-year-old man recollected one time he was hiking with his peers up in Alaska, he once experienced hypothermia due to cold weather. He was almost declared dead. In his mind, after the second experience, he still believed, "he was not supposed to be here." As we mentioned earlier, the question, "what would you tell the world if you have sixty seconds to live?" exposes the present mindset of the person who is answering the question. Clearly the survivor's mindset would be "I was not supposed to be here." The part of the question that calls for self-inventory would still elicit the same response. And finally, the third nuance of the question, which is to cause one to take action, would likely not be acknowledged or acted upon by the survivor, as he would feel no obligation to take action. Living life from the rearview mirror cripples us from self-actualization; it prevents us from making our own positive contribution to the world, or more simply it betrays our own obligation to our own lives. —This book is about us searching through our souls and minds to find purpose. What would be our answer to the question, "What would you tell the world if you have sixty seconds to live?" Whatever our answers are, let us start living in the now because we cannot predict what the next second brings. Let us not live like the man in his sixties who still believes that "he is not supposed to be here." Living life without regret is living a life of gratitude. If we find it difficult to cope with this question or to understand its depth, seeking for clarification from those we look up to might be a great start.

The Importance of Having Mentors

A recent study emphasizes the importance of mentors in life-changing situations, suggesting that "Mentors are crucial whenever people are faced with new phases of their career or life that require the development of new knowledge, skills or attitudes." Everyone, be it teenagers, adults, professionals, elderly, etc., needs a mentor. Nobody is above having a mentor. Mentoring is a mark of growth and humility. In other words, seeking a mentor is an indication that we are teachable Finding a mentor in any concentration is a great approach to personal and professional development. What it means to ponder what we would tell the world if we had one minute to live might be a moot question if we don't know why we are here in the first place. Seeking clarification is a strength, not a weakness. Some people may not have a sense of purpose, making it difficult to know what to tell to the world. Based on research, seeking clarification or enlightenment is critical in answering the why and how of life. If we can see our goals clearly, we can pursue them constructively. And if we can pursue them constructively, we can be confident enough to share our knowledge with others who need it.

Finding mentors can be a challenge, because mentoring has so many facets, depending on the area of concern. Acquiring the appropriate mentor is easier if three criteria are met.

Purpose of mentorship

First of all, in order for mentoring to be effective, there must be a clear understanding of why mentoring is needed: personal development, career development, spiritual development, etc.

J. Ibeh Agbanyim

When the purpose of obtaining a mentor is defined, then it is easier to focus on specifics.

Specific Area for mentorship

Being specific is always a good approach to self-improvement. For example, if we are looking for mentoring in the area of personal development, it might be more specific to define personal development as "goal-setting." With this specification in mind, we can formulate the appropriate questions for our mentor. Personal development is a lifelong process as it has so many layers to address; so, start with specifics and build confidence from there. After dealing with specifics, be prepared and willing to apply those strategies mentors recommend. One strategy is to seek information; another is to apply information as necessary.

Willingness to Apply Lessons Learned

Information without translation has no practical value. Information is useful when translated and applied. For example, after receiving information on goal setting, the next thing to do is to start setting goals on how to improve personally. Without application, the information received becomes dormant and unproductive. Therefore, in order to utilize mentoring, it is critical to translate the information received into results. Only when information is translated will it become useful and relevant. The goal of having a mentor should be focused on application of lessons learned from the mentor. As we grow in whatever area of interest, it becomes easier to answer the question "what would you tell the world if you have sixty seconds to live?"

Some of us, in the wee hours or when we are alone, tend to ponder why we are here. What is the purpose of our existence? What have we contributed to ourselves and society? How will we be remembered? What legacy are we living behind? There can be other mind-boggling questions as well. An American Psychological Association research study led by psychologist Joseph Ferrari, PhD found that twenty percent of U.S. men and women are chronic procrastinators. "They delay at home, work, school, and in relationships." On the other hand, the study also mentioned that "non-procrastinators focus on the task that needs to be done. They have a stronger personal identity and are less concerned about what psychologists call "social esteem"—how others like us—as opposed to self-esteem which is how we feel about ourselves." (American Psychological Association, 2010). In the final analysis, we should live life in the now and enjoy ourselves, rather than delay or deflect because of fears or insecurities. Are we among the twenty percent who procrastinate or are we one of those who take action? This might be a personal decision and reflection moment. Live life to the fullest that we may be able to have a message to tell to the world in sixty seconds.

The next chapter discusses the question "Why not me?" We are familiar with people often asking "Why me?" particularly when they are going through challenges and difficulties. When we offer up this rhetorical question, we are essentially saying we would rather have this situation happen to somebody else. This chapter sets out to reverse the question. If it's not me, then who? Hopefully, this chapter will lead readers to understand that each time we take such an attitude we are positioning ourselves for self-pity and distorted reasoning and are being emotionally absent. Instead, when we take ownership of the situation, we tend to find solutions to the challenges as opposed to blaming others or feeling victimized. On the other hand, when we witness others helping the needy or volunteering in any way, we tend to justify their actions but yet we never make ourselves available in the same way. This chapter hopefully will help us develop the spirit of volunteering selflessly, and turn our individualism into collaboration and inclusion—for a common purpose of uplifting humanity.

Notes

American Psychological Association. 2010. *Psychology of Procrastination: Why People Put Off Important Tasks Until the Last Minute*, http://www.apa.org/news/press/releases/2010/04/procrastination.aspx

Stringer, H. 2016. Monitor on Psychology. *"The life-changing power of mentors."* A publication of the American Psychological Association, June 26. Vol. 47. No. 6, p. 54.

Vickers, A. 2011. *People vs. the State of Illusion*. Exalt Film.

Chapter 8

Why Not Me?

You change your life when you change
your mind.
—Jim Stovall

Jim Stovall is one of the most influential change agents of our time. His lifetime achievements attest to the wealth of work he is contributing to humanity. His message is all about helping people realize their dreams and living a successful life. His famous quote "you change your life when you change your mind" remains foundational to his body of work. Growing up, he faced what an average person would consider devastating: he went completely blind. Remarkably, he turned his circumstances into an oasis of opportunities simply by applying his methodology of "you change your life when you change your mind." Jim Stovall used his disability as a catalyst in assisting millions of visually impaired people by co-founding the Narrative Television Network (NTN), "which makes movies and television accessible for our nation's 13 million blind and visually impaired people and their families." He won an Emmy Award for his contribution. His life journey is chronicled in his book "The Way I See the World," published in 1999. Since its publication, Jim has published a total of twenty-six books. Jim turned his personal tragedy into possibility for others. His approach teaches us how to celebrate life on a daily basis, despite our challenges. He is the epitome of courage in action.

How we celebrate life depends on how we show up. Our daily perceptions determine what we make of life that particular day. It is not what happens to us that matter. It is our opinion and attitude toward what happens to us that matters. For example, waking up in the morning after a bad dream does not necessarily mean our entire day is ruined. Waking up to another day is in itself a new beginning. It is a golden opportunity to define and create your desired experience. Celebrate the day with affirmation and gratitude. It is an opportunity to demonstrate our talents, gifts, and kindnesses unto others. A simple mind shift can change the way we view our life and circumstances. We all deserve a second chance in life, a fresh start, whether on the receiving or giving end. Dr. Maya Angelou profoundly said, "No matter how heinous a crime, if a human being did it, I have to say I have in me all the components that are in her, or in him—I intend to use my energies constructively as opposed to destructively." We choose to use our energy either constructively or destructively. John Newton, former seventeenth century slave runner, is a primary example of an individual who turned his tortured life experience around and wrote the most widely sung hymn in the world, "Amazing Grace."

There is a point in our lives when taking responsibility is noble. And the sooner we come to this realization, the sooner we live a full life. By understanding the urgency of asking "Why not me?" we begin to see our circumstances as opportunities rather than dead ends. Whenever unforeseen circumstances happen, we are quick to ask, "Why me?" It is a question that implies defeat, illustrating a victim, instead of a victor, mentality. We must attempt to acknowledge that it is a privilege to be breathing and having experiences at all, as opposed to wishing our misfortune would happen to others. Embracing our challenges and taking pride in overcoming our difficulties is a sign of maturity and strength. "Why not me?" speaks to the very essence of taking control of our situations. Jim Stovall's experience is an example of the efficacy of saying "Why not me?" He turned his story around by taking control of his life and doing something about his situation. He touched millions of people by simply embracing his dreams and aspirations. His actions and tenacity are a testament to his achievement. We challenge you today to embrace your dreams, and apply your utmost strength toward becoming your utmost self.

The danger of short-changing ourselves with regard to our own potential is that we rob countless people of the opportunity to learn from our expertise, our gifts, and our experience. If there is anyone who can create a cure for HIV, "why not me?" If there is anybody who can lend a helping hand to a homeless, "Why not me?" If there is anybody who has the insight to improve marriages and other human relationships, "Why not me?" If there is anybody who can strive to end global violence, "Why not me?" If there is anybody who can show a little kindness to neighbors, co-workers, colleagues, and orphans, "Why not me?" The world is waiting for people of goodwill to share the message of peace, love, diversity and inclusion. Why can't any one of us be that person? Mahatma Gandhi said "You must be the change you want to see in the world." Every time we fail to do right, we rob humanity of the most precious gift of caring for one another. Every time that we blame others for societal abnormalities, we rob humanity of forgiveness. When we as individuals or as a group refuse to show kindness to others, we contribute to the demise of our existence. This book is a call for action. We should not wait for tragedy to occur before we do what we know is the right thing; kindness can never go out of fashion. If every one of us answers the call of humanity and thinks "Why can't I be the one who makes this day a good day, for myself and others? We as people are holding one another hostage, and until we understand this, humanity will hold all of us accountable for not delivering kindness and mercy to all.

In a city of half a million people, if everyone says "thank you" after eating a meal, either at home or in a restaurant, it would be newsworthy. There would be a pandemic, noticeable change in the mood of the populus. If we doubt this ominous exercise, start by sharing the message with friends and family members. Eventually, each and every one of us will partake in making our city the healthiest city in America. It starts with each and every one of us expressing gratitude. If we can make a commitment to take individual responsibility without worrying whether we are politically correct or not, our environment will change positively. The Dalai Lama once said "If every eight-year-old in the world is taught meditation, we will eliminate violence from the world within one generation." This shows the strength of positively learning from one another. It would be gratifying to participate in eliminating violence within one generation. The idea of collaborative effort is energizing and harmonious. The application relies on individual and collective commitment—and if anybody can contribute in making this world a better place by one act of kindness at a time, "Why not me?" The next chapter discusses The Three Dimensions of a Complete Life. This powerful message was first presented by Dr. Martin Luther King Jr. at New Covenant Baptist Church in Chicago. The message is relevant and ageless. The reason for including this chapter is to get us thinking how the three dimensions highlighted apply in our own lives. Our lives are out of balance if we do not align with these three dimensions.

The next chapter will use evidence-based studies and practical stories to validate the application of these three dimensions and how they apply in today's life experience.

J. Ibeh Agbanyim

Notes

Edberg, H. (2013). *Gandhi's 10 Rules for Changing the World*, http://www.dailygood.org/story/466/gandhi-s-10-rules-for-changing-the-world-henrik-edberg/

Gluskin, D. (2013). *Meditation, Demystified*, http://www.huffingtonpost.com/dawn-gluskin/meditation_b_2382626.html

Jiaquan Xu, Sherry L. Murphy, Kenneth, D. Kochanek; and Brigham, A. Bastian. (2016). National Vital Statistics Reports: Deaths: Final Data for 2013, http://www.cdc.gov/nchs/data/nvsr/nvsr64/nvsr64_02.pdf

OWN TV. The Lesson Dr. Maya Angelou Is Still Studying in Her 80s- Oprah's Master Class-OWN, https://www.youtube.com/watch?v=N8RA4JsoKjY

Stovall, J. (1999). *The Way I See My World*. United States of America, Companion Enterprises Inc.

Chapter 9

The Three Dimensions of a Complete Life

If you get, give. If you learn, teach.
—Dr. Maya Angelou

The Three Dimensions of Life as presented by Dr. Martin Luther King Jr. are the Length, Breadth, and Height of life. In order to live a complete life, these three dimensions should be in concert. While this chapter borrows the title from Dr. King Jr.'s 1967 message at New Covenant Baptist Church in Chicago, the goal is to relate the message to the twenty-first century way of life. We will draw from research and anecdotes on how to live a complete life using this approach. The intent of this chapter is also to encourage human relationships and promote diversity and inclusion.

It is difficult to feel another person's pain if we have never been in that person's shoes. Empathy speaks to the very essence of shared experience. For example, anyone who has suffered the loss of a parent, child, spouse, or other loved one can empathize with others' losses. Anyone who suffers from addiction can empathize with the drug problems of others. The pain is even deeper when we are self-aware. In other words, understanding ourselves, what

65

J. Ibeh Agbanyim

makes us tick, makes us feel for others when we see others going through similar emotions. Self-efficacy is critical in the journey of life. It also helps in how we relate to one another. Dr. Martin Luther King Jr. calls it the "Length" of life.

When we are aware of our own pains, joy, and happiness it is easier to feel the pains, joy, and happiness of others. Even if we do not know the other person intimately or otherwise, the fact that they are human beings like ourselves is enough to relate to them. To restate it simply, "love thy neighbor as thyself." Our neighbors, in a broader context, are people whom we come in contact with on a daily basis, whether in the workplace or in social settings. Dr.King calls treating people how we want to be treated "Breadth" of life.

When we make efforts to understand ourselves, it is easier to extend the same understanding to others. And when we have the capacity to understand others, it is possible and practical to connect with a power that is higher than ourselves. Higher power speaks of a spiritual realm—power that is greater than our understanding but yet has presence in what we do on a daily basis. Higher power has nothing to do with religion; instead it has everything to do with spirituality. When we come to a place where we can connect with spirituality, then we have come to communion with that third dimension that Dr. King calls the "Height" of life.

The Length of Life

Sports psychologist and certified hypnotherapist Dr. Sam Sterk states in his book, WIN! Get The Mental Edge Skills in Martial Arts, that our thoughts, emotions and feelings drive how martial artists perform during competition and belt promotion. Internal verbal behavior is more important than any knowledge a competitor acquires. In other words, the stories we tell ourselves make a world of difference in how we perform in an arena. And people see us the way we see ourselves. There is an urgent need and a call to action for us to ask ourselves the question, "Who am I?" Our entire existence and success in life is determined by the way we answer this question. As a child, we believe that everything is possible. But as we grow older, we start to allow destructive fear to permeate the way we see ourselves and the world. This distorted self-report follows us throughout our lives. It becomes critical that we reevaluate views about ourselves periodically. One way to measure a child's intelligence or how they understand their world is through exposing them to a variety of intelligence environments. This exposure can reveal the child's area of interest and their communication skills. Dr. Kathy Koch's 8 Great Smarts discusses the eight types of intelligences, and how important it is for parents, guardians, and caregivers to pay attention to how children learn through the lenses of word smart, logic smart, picture smart, music smart, body smart, nature smart, people smart, and self smart, as popularized by Dr. Tom Armstrong. The book suggests that children learn based on their type(s) of intelligences. For example, some children learn better when words are presented to them. This means whenever they are exposed to reading words or letters, their brains capture the information more efficiently and they learn at a faster rate. Some children learn through logic, which means asking questions. Others learn through be exposed to nature, i.e. parks, gardens, etc. It is important that we understand our mode of interpreting the world. Applying this in adult lives, it is critical that we understand who we are, and what makes us interesting a whole. Knowing thyself is the first step to living a complete or "length" of life. To further this discussion on the Length of life, how well do we know ourselves? Can we really claim that we know ourselves properly? What evidence can we show to validate our claim?

Jewish Rabbi, Dr. Joshua L. Liebman in his book, Peace of Mind, encourages us to love ourselves properly—not a narcissistic type of self-love. Proper self-love is foundational and shows in the way we interact with one another. While there is statistical evidence to support that suicides can be rooted in mental disorder and illness, suicide is also an indication of low self-esteem. Sadly, the American Foundation for Suicide Prevention reports that in 2013, 42,773 Americans died by suicide, making suicide the tenth leading cause of death in the United States. Suicide costs the United States forty-four billion dollars annually. "Love for oneself is the foundation of a brotherly society and personal peace of mind," (Liebman, 1994). The benefit of exercising peace of mind has a spillover effect. It encourages healthy human relationships irrespective of demographics. It is when we love ourselves properly so that we can love others the same.

The Breadth of Life

If the length of life (self-love) is not met, it is difficult to love others in healthy ways. A society's health meter is a measurement of the love or hate levels of the society. In other words, before a society can achieve healthy human relationships, proper self-love is critical. So how can we measure our societal health? By beginning with how we treat one another. We need look no further than ourselves, because we as individuals are testaments to the health of our environment. Dr. King called it the "Breadth" of life. For us to meet the breadth of life, we should strive to care for one another with an unbiased mindset. When we apply the length of life and breadth of life, we are getting closer to achieving the "Height" of life. The height of life speaks to our relationship with a higher power. How we measure the breadth of life is deep-seated in how we take care of others who cross our paths.

We may ask ourselves, when was the last time we gave a helping hand to our neighbors? When was the last time we offered help to our co-workers even when they appeared to be doing fine? Offered to babysit for a struggling single mother, so she could perhaps look for a job or just to give her some time to herself? Or offered our reference to an applicant who was looking for work? Gave listening ears to a young adult seeking counsel? Volunteered at an orphanage, shelter, or food bank? The list goes on how we can measure our breadth of life or our relationships with other people, especially non-family members. When we partake in any of these altruistic events on a regular basis, we are positioning ourselves to "living a complete life." It is a conscious effort worth exploring because, in the long run, our small contribution adds to a greater cause, which is to live in a balanced society. It takes discipline, conscious decision-making, commitment, hard work, and spiritual intelligence to achieve a complete life. And it starts with taking care of one another, irrespective of demographics. Location does not affect our pains nor our joys. Emotions are universal. We are interrelated and interconnected by our humanity.

The Height of Life

Tragedy has a way of calling our attention to what matters. Health crises have a way of exposing our weaknesses and strengths. Life's problems have a way of revealing our connection to humanity and our spirituality. The "height" of life in this context narrates how spiritually connected and stable we are in pursuit of a complete life. The height of life speaks to how relatable we are when we experience challenges, whether positive or negative.

9-11 Experience

September 11, 2001 was the worst day in the United States history. It was a tragedy that shook citizens to the core. It affected global economy, and most importantly, humanity was tested. The idea of two fully fueled aircrafts crashing into the Twin Towers at the World Trade Center was unthinkable. The awful magnitude of the event brought all Americans and others across the globe to a reality check. Firefighters, first responders, and ordinary citizens scrambled to assist in any way possible without worrying for their own safety. Nobody was worried about who was Christian or non-Christian, believer or non-believer, male or female, young or old, Republican or Democrat. None of those categorical and denominational barriers mattered at that particular moment. What mattered was we were humans experiencing human trauma and death. The levels of collaboration and togetherness experienced during that crisis were a record indicator and predictor of "what affects one directly, affects all indirectly." Thousands looked for a way to assist the victims of 9/11 by traveling from coast-to-coast to help at Ground Zero. Pastors, imams, ordinary citizens, did everything they could. There were vigils held all across the nation as a sign of support. The outpouring of sympathy for those affected was universal. In times such as that September morning, people seek spiritual comfort and peace—a universal and internal peace that surpasses all understanding—reaching out to what some call God, while others call it different names. The bottom line is that people seek answers beyond human understanding. It is when we reach at that level of helplessness and consciousness that our true humanity to connect to higher power is exposed. Different life events lead people to that level of space—divorce, loss of loved ones, sickness, massive success, birth of a baby, and so forth. These are examples of what pushes people to reach the third dimension, the "Height" of life. All human beings have the capacity to experience these three dimensions. This is an individual quest. If we really want to experience a complete life, all three dimensions have to be achieved.

Recap

The three dimensions of a complete life are part of a human quest. It is also an individual pursuit. In order to experience a complete life, we must as individuals long to achieve these three dimensions. First, before we can love or have deep care for another human being, we must first love self properly, i.e. "length" of life. Loving one's self properly suggest that we understand ourselves on a deep level: what makes us who we are, what are our strengths and weaknesses. . Only when we achieve this goal of loving ourselves can we attempt to love others the same way.

Second, in order to live a complete life, we must reach the "breadth" of life. The breadth of life reflects on loving our neighbors as we love ourselves. It is a personal decision to love and care for others. It is not a corporate agenda, or a collective pursuit. It is a personal commitment to endeavor to treat others equally. The idea of waiting for a group to care for another group before making our personal decision leads to group-think, and group-think does not represent the true meaning of the "Length of Life." The way we love our neighbors is an indication of how we love ourselves. One must marry length of life with the breadth of life. When we do this, it is easier to pursue the height of life. Finally, the height of life depicts our ability to connect to a higher power. A higher power is that force that we cannot explain or describe, but we feel or know somehow exists. It involves those significant experiences where the end result cannot be explained logically. For example, 9/11 demonstrated how people came together for solidarity and support, reaching to a higher power rather than succumbing to their own fears or prejudices. Times of various crises in our lives are when we are the most liable to reach out and attain the height of life.

The next chapter discusses The Three Types of Ignorance. Understanding ignorance in its various forms will help us be aware of how we conduct ourselves in different situations. We will thus be able to self-monitor how we treat others and catch ourselves when we are succumbing to one or more forms of ignorance. We will be encouraged to differentiate among the characteristics and effects of the levels of ignorance.

Notes

Agbanyim, J. I. (2013). Fear: A Figment of Our Imagination. In *Fear: A Healthy Emotion If Well Managed* (1st ed., p. 3) Bloomington, Indiana. iUniverse.

American Foundation for Suicide Prevention (2014). Suicide Statistic, http://afsp.org/about-suicide/suicide-statistics/

Geller, S. (2005). What's on your mind? Thinking is critical to people-based safety(TM). ISHN, 39(9), 21-21,23. Retrieved from http://search.proquest.com/docview/196525310?accountid=35812

Koch, K. (2016). *8 Great Smarts: Discover and Nurture Your Child's Intelligence*. Chicago. Moody Publishers

Liebman, L. L. (1994). *Peace of Mind: Insights on Human Nature that can Change your Life*. New York, N.Y. Carol Publishing.

Martin Luther King, Jr. And The Global Freedom Struggle: The Three Dimensions of a Complete Life, http://kingencyclopedia.stanford.edu/encyclopedia/documentsentry/doc_the_three_dimensions_of_a_complete_life.1.html

Sterk, S. (2016). *Win! Get The Mental Edge Skills in Martial Arts: Improved Martial Arts Performance with Mental Skill Training*. CreateSpace Independent Publishing Platform

Chapter 10

Three Types of Ignorance

Science is like looking for a black cat in a
dark room, and there may not be a cat in
the room.

—Stuart Firestein

The highest mountain any human being can scale is the mountain of ignorance. Ignorance as generally perceived can handicap or paralyze our thoughts and actions. Nobody is above ignorance. No genius, specialist, or expert can claim an ignorance-free life. There is always something that we are ignorant about. The acknowledgement that no one is above ignorance is the beginning of self-discovery and development. It is admission or ownership that liberates and opens doors of opportunities. It is the beginning of wisdom when we confidently and humbly admit what we don't know it all. Anything ever discovered was discovered on the heels of admitting ignorance and doing something to be informed. Research is based on admitting ignorance; personal growth is based on admitting lack of knowledge in a particular area.

Technological advancement is built around a quest for knowledge and escape from dogma.

Ignorance is constructive and effective when embraced and turned into practical and positive results. Many discoveries came into existence as a result of a quest for knowledge. This chapter will present ignorance from a glorified and dignified perspective. In other words, ignorance is beneficial when we admit and understand the three types of ignorance: ordinary, willful, and higher. Understanding the different forms of ignorance allows us to pre-select the level on which to operate—whether to operate on the premise of uplifting humanity or attacking humanity. For example, a medical doctor has mastered the fundamentals of medicine in a particular area, but still cannot claim absolute knowledge of medicine; an attorney has a wealth of knowledge in a particular area of jurisprudence, but cannot claim absolute knowledge of the law. A mother of three children who raises her children in a healthy environment cannot claim an absolute knowledge of child rearing. A husband who loves his wife cannot claim absolute knowledge of marital relationships; instead he's eager to learn from others who have been in relationships longer. A student who graduates from a program cannot claim absolute knowledge on the other programs the university offers. While we claim knowledge in one particular area, we are also ignorant in other areas. The understanding that no matter how much we know, we will never know it all is a beginning of living a free and peaceful life. There is no shame in admitting lack of knowledge in a particular area of discipline or training, or even in a conversation. It simply suggests that we are teachable.

In an effort to explain each one of the three types of ignorance, it is critical to pay attention to practical examples associated with each of them and relate them in our lives.

J. Ibeh Agbanyim

Ordinary Ignorance

Ordinary ignorance is the fundamental premise that nobody knows it all. It means that we seek direction in a particular issue at hand. For example, an invitation for a job interview requires that the applicant show up twenty minutes early. We apply ordinary ignorance when we map out directions on how to get to the interview location days before by using GPS, and also anticipate travel time during rush hour. Failure to take this simple inventory could cause the applicant to show up late or miss the interview entirely. Either option is not a good first impression. A thinking thing to do is to be prepared. The beauty about understanding ordinary ignorance is that it is the most common mistake we tend to make: assuming things are "no big deal." Yet, missing a job interview can raise a red flag to the interviewer. In this context, ordinary ignorance is moving from not knowing to knowing, which is "the very essence of learning." To humanize this kind of ignorance, when we meet a person of different background or ethnicity, the humane thing to do is to get to know them by introducing ourselves and carrying on a decent conversation. In the process of the conversation, we get to know each other better. The wrong approach in getting to know a person is by starting a conversation focused on a person's ethnicity, nationality, race, religion etc., because that will establish the tone of the conversation. In other words, every other word uttered will likely evolve around that person's nationality, ethnicity, religion, race etc., rather than deal with the person as a human being, by starting a conversation from the simple premise of making introductions and small talk, the atmosphere is humanized without putting anyone on the defensive. Ordinary ignorance in essence moves an experience from not knowing to knowing. And when once we know, we cannot claim ignorance of that particular information we have just learned.

Willful Ignorance

Willful ignorance is after knowing about something, we pretend like we do not know it at all. In other words, it is a conscious and calculated ignorance. This kind of ignorance can be very dangerous. A professor at Columbia University, Dr. Stuart Firestein calls it "willful stupidity,"which is "worse than simple stupidity, it is callow indifference to facts or logic." The danger of willful stupidity or willful ignorance is, "it shows itself as a stubborn devotion to uninformed opinions, ignoring (same root) contrary ideas, opinions, or data."

A practical example of willful ignorance would be asking employees or management within a workplace to falsify data in order to make the Sales Department look like top performers. The result is an environment of mistrust and fear. Every employee knows that it is wrong, but no one will speak out for fear of the consequences of being singled out within the group. In a marriage, when a spouse knows what will start an argument in a relationship but continues to "go there," it creates acrimony and chaos in the relationship. Willful ignorance is the root cause of family and societal dysfunction. When an individual knows the best thing to do in order to maintain peace, but decides not to do it due to peer pressure, groupthink, complacency, or other hidden agendas, willful ignorance has been committed. It takes a person with character, integrity, honesty, authenticity and vigor to admit willful stupidity and retract from living a willfully ignorant life. The third of level of ignorance is called Higher Ignorance.

J. Ibeh Agbanyim

Higher Ignorance

Higher ignorance is where research and discoveries happen. It speaks volumes about a person or a group when we operate using higher ignorance. "A higher ignorance allows us to be open and curious in the face of knowing that we do not know." Higher ignorance is the understanding that, no matter how much we know as intellects or human beings, we will never know it all. It is a kind of ignorance that not only brings curiosity; it also encourages humility. Any person or group who operates in this capacity understands the importance of humility and the art of listening. Higher ignorance exposes a person to a place of wonderment and adventure. It is the opiate of imagination and discovery. Anything ever discovered was discovered as a result of higher ignorance— the desire to know more.

Viagra! The Unexpected Discovery

Viagra was discovered while scientists were experimenting with medication to cure hypertension or high blood pressure. "During the clinical trials, researchers discovered that the drug was more effective at inducing erection than treating angina." After the Food and Drug Administration (FDA) approved Viagra, it reached record sales levels of close to $2 billion in 2008. Studies show that in United States alone, an estimated thirty million men, and seventy million men worldwide suffer from Erectile Dysfunction (ED). And by acting on the new information, a cure for ED was discovered.

Higher ignorance has helped scientists solve the world's great puzzles. Ignorance rightly channeled brings light, hope and healing to the world. We should never discount the power of well-channeled ignorance, because not all ignorance is negative and detrimental. Dismissing new information can inhibit imagination and creativity, therefore prohibiting discovery.

In his book Ignorance: How it Drives Science, Dr. Firestein puts it succinctly: "Science is like looking for a black cat in a dark room, and there may not be a cat in the room." Higher ignorance allows us to look again to the familiar. We may find new versions of an old story. Therefore, we should not underestimate the potency of information. If nothing else, at least take time to entertain new information, even if we are likely to discard it, because we could find something we never anticipated. Meeting a person for the first time can cause a sense of unease and distorted expectations—in some cases fear of the unknown. But higher ignorance allows us to approach such friendship or initial introduction with curiosity and an open mind. When we approach one another with open minds we can find out holistic information about ourselves. Coming into a situation with preconceived notions, prejudices or biases, we operate under willful ignorance. Remember, willful ignorance refers to approaching life with pretense and closed-mindedness. For a transformation to take place, we should move our thought processes from willful stupidity to higher ignorance. In this state, we allow ourselves to "entertain new information without necessarily believing or accepting it." To get to this level of thinking, there are three practical ways to challenge our thinking when entertaining information from different types of ignorance perspectives.

J. Ibeh Agbanyim

Three Practical Ways to Challenge our Thinking

Exercise Soul-searching

One of the most powerful things we can do when we become overwhelmed is to self-report, self- inventory, self-evaluate or in another word, soul-search. Soul searching is where we come face to face with our conscience. Our conscience is where reality meets illusion. In order to get a clear inventory of ourselves, we can exercise soul-searching, and think through our life journey. We can ask hard questions such as "How did I get here?" "Where do I go from here?" and "Who am I?" When we come to this space in our lives, it allows us to self-examine and be brutally honest with ourselves. In the process of answering life-challenging questions, we discover ourselves in a very intimate atmosphere, and most importantly, we acquire a degree of humility. This exercise requires higher thinking.

Avoid Willful Ignorance

In order to be true to self, we ought to avoid pretense and finger pointing or blaming games. When we refrain from willful ignorance, we become more serious and committed to seeking practical answers to troubling questions. Avoiding willful ignorance allows us to face the issue as opposed to entertaining the symptoms. To get to root cause, critical thinking is required. We should distance ourselves from entertaining willful ignorance because it cripples our thought processes when we pretend or blame others for our issues. Instead, when we are face-to-face with our problems it is easier to seek practical solutions and prevent negative results.

Response vs. Reaction Approach

It is always advisable to learn how to respond to situations rather than react to them. Responding to situations requires a critical and thorough thinking approach. Responding to issues of the heart requires active listening and patience. On the other hand, reacting to situations require minimal thinking and in most cases leads to shallow results. In order to operate on higher ignorance frequency, critical thinking is important as well as open-mindedness and curiosity.

Understanding the three types of ignorance will allow us to re-examine the way we communicate with one another—most importantly, the way we conduct internal verbal behaviors. When our internal constituents are at peace, it will radiate through the way we communicate within our environments. We should ask ourselves how are we handling our conduct with regard to these three types of ignorance, and which of the three is dominating in our behavior? Hopefully, the more we ponder the three levels of ignorance, the better equipped we become when interacting with one another.

The next chapter is entitled You Are Not Alone. "No man is an island," wrote John Donne. We are all connected to the elements we come in contact with. It took a team and series of events for us to find ourselves on this planet. To go through life discounting or ignoring the fact that we arrived here through the help of others can cause us to live a life of discontent, denial, ingratitude, and all the negative energies associated with shallow thinking and narrow-mindedness. Hopefully, this chapter will help us to understand that we are relevant, interrelated and need each other to make this world a better place. Demographics are not as important as understanding that we are all human beings who share the same psychological needs. Human physiological needs are universal.

Notes

Anderson, L. 2016. *How a Little Pill Changed the World*, https://www.drugs.com/slideshow/the-rise-to-fame-viagra-and-erectile-dysfunction-1043

Firestein, S. 2012. *Ignorance: How It Drives Science*. New York: Oxford University Press.

Smalley, S. L. (2011). *Willful Ignorance: Penn State and "Don't Ask, Don't Tell."* Retrieved from, http://www.psychologytoday.com/blog/look-around-and-look-within/201111/willful-ignorance-penn-state-and-dont-ask-dont-tell

Chapter 11

You Are Not Alone

There are certain undeniable truths in the universe when it comes to the human race. There are truths that remind us that we have never been alone. Right from the beginning, we have always been linked to the source or channel that brought us into this world. And through that channel remains evidence that we are never alone. Even in death, someone has to prepare our bodies for burial, cremation, or any other means necessary to put our souls at peace. These are some of the undisputable and unapologetic truths about human existence:

- We were all born naked
- Somebody cared and clothed us in some fashion or another when we were babies
- Pain and joy have universal psychological affects
- Someone must have assisted us to arrive at where we are at this moment
- Every human being has blood that runs in their veins (no exceptions)

These truths are the same across the seven continents of the world. Therefore, they are universal truths. If we come to life with this mindset, it is then we can relate to one another on levels that depict humanity. It is not how intelligent we are that defines our humanity. It is not how tall, short, handsome, or beautiful we are that defines our humanity. Instead, the undeniable and undisputable universal constructs listed above are living proof that we are not alone. To embrace these truths is to respect one another irrespective of culture, religion, gender, and other demographical identifications that sometimes work against us. There are several life examples that support this claim that we are never alone. While the focus of this chapter is to encourage us that we are not ever alone, it is critical to note that we are all mirrors: reflections of what we see or perceive. In other words, when we look in a mirror, if we see ourselves as inadequate, incompetent, unfit, or ugly, we tend to portray the same negativity toward another person. This feeling of unworthiness permeates the way we treat one another, especially people who we have no direct relationship with. On the other hand, when we see ourselves clearly and optimistically, it radiates through our interactions and our deeds. The message of consciousness is to understand that we are more alike than unalike. It is on this human foundation that we share this chapter. It is also important to understand that whenever we are angry, we are essentially afraid of something. Anger is just a channel that we use to communicate our masks. The next time that we are angry about something or somebody, ask ourselves, "What are we afraid of?" If we can pinpoint what it is that frightens or intimidates us, we can then channel our anger and energy to fix whatever challenges we face. To dwell on perpetual negative energy is an indication of lack of self-discipline, self-efficacy, internal verbal behavior, and distorted perception. Because life will always present difficult and challenging situations from time to time, the earlier we learn how to control ourselves, the earlier we overcome our destructive fears.

Destructive fears are those emotions that can lead us to make poor decisions, judgments, and reach hasty conclusions which eventually create further tensions.

People who understand these concepts live lives of compassion, grace, gratitude and love for one another. They face their fears by channeling their anger into doing good and making positive contributions as opposed to fleeing from humanity in fear of untested assumptions. This thought process breaks demographic barriers and positions a person to live a life of consciousness and altruism. When we embrace life with this attitude we can assist people, not because of our business or personal relationships, but purely because of our humanity. "We are not alone" translates into "what affects one directly, affects all indirectly." The next paragraph discusses a real life experience about two men from different cultures who share the thread of humanity.

A Stranger Donated His Kidney to a Kidney Patient

A true story about a kidney recipient and a surprising donor in 2015 demonstrates the concept of "We are not alone." A man who barely knew a patient who needed a kidney decided to donate his own organ. The recipient was incredulous: it was inconceivable that someone without strong emotional or familial ties would want to make such a sacrifice. Both men were from different cultural backgrounds. They did however share the same birthday and were both married with children. The purpose of this anecdote is to demonstrate that, while the organ recipient worried over the possibility of finding a donor, the universe rearranged itself to send a generous person to donate one of his kidneys. Help can come from a place we least expect. We encourage readers to read more about this story by researching the reference attached. The important thing is that we are not alone in this space called life—

even those who claim to be self-made have interactions and assistance in some form that revolutionized their thought processes. Overtime, history has shown that mankind has always wanted to create divisiveness among its various sects. Time and time again, however, the universe reminds us that we are not alone. We are in essence interrelated, interconnected and more similar, irrespective of our geographical locations and boundaries. If nothing else, borders, inequality and inequity have made humanity more cruel, indifferent, discriminating, and hateful. During a TV interview an astronaut made an interesting observation, as was told by world-renowned artist Yanni, during a concert in the Acropolis of Athens, Greece.

There are No Physical Borders in the Airspace

Renowned instrumentalist Yanni performed a live concert at the Acropolis over two decades ago. Toward the end of his show, he narrated a story about an astronaut who was being interviewed by the media about his experience in space. He related that when cruising over Europe in the space shuttle, he noticed that he could not tell European countries apart because there were no physical borders that separated them. At that moment it dawned on him that the universe was not created with borders and walls that demarcate countries or continents, but that people created those borders for control. In airspace, there are no such things as physical borders; instead, people created imaginary lines whereby creating division which further creates classism, abuse of power, inequality, inequity, and the withholding of resources from one group to another. Yet, when world crises and unrest happen, heads of state will scramble for allies to assist in balancing power and keeping world peace—an indication that we are not alone. It is of great importance to note that if humans can see life through the lenses of humanity instead of selfishness and callousness, humanity will be better than it is now. But the mind-shift starts with individual responsibility and accountability. In other words, the most powerful weapon available to mankind is self-control, willpower, and the courage to do right even in the face of opposition.

To ignore the belief that we are not alone in this universe is to promote violence, division, discrimination, classism, abuse of power, and a host of other social disruptions that are associated with man's inhumanity to man. There are three yardsticks worth sharing to further discussion on the concept that "we are not alone."

Self-Editing

It is a human desire to portray oneself as amiable, intelligent, confident, and humane. This internal urge to do everything right shows in the way we speak in public, comport ourselves, or address one another in a public atmosphere. It also shows in the way we communicate with written words when presenting a report to our bosses or our superiors. We demonstrate this sensitivity through editing our thoughts after writing, which is called self-editing. The same principle applies when we pause and think before speaking. For us to understand "we are not alone," we have to self-edit our thoughts, perceptions, judgments, skepticisms, and biases. It is when we process our thoughts critically that we understand the importance of believing that we are not alone.

Needing Help When We Are Sick

Sickness cripples the strong as well as the weak. Sickness disrupts our concentration, performance, and peace. Sickness does not discriminate. Sickness has a universal psychological influence on the body. When sickness engulfs us, it takes a team to help us recover. A team could be our partner who cares enough to take us to the drug store, hospital, or other such facility. In our sick beds, the only thing that matters is our well being. Doctors, nurses, nurse aides, even janitors, contribute in their big and small ways in restoring our health. It validates this idea of "no one is an island." If we can remember how it feels to be sick and helpless, we will empathize with anyone who finds themselves in the same sort of pain or discomfort.

Having a Sense of Accomplishment

There is a universal behavior we exhibit when our loved ones excel or accomplish a task. Sometimes, we share our excitement with someone whom we hardly know. For example, when we see a baby on TV smiling and playing joyously, we will mirror the joy in our own expressions. We usually smile in a universal appreciation of youthful innocence, connecting with the infant on a human or moral level. According to Yale professor of psychology Dr. Paul Bloom, in his book Just Babies, "We have a moral sense that enables us to judge others and that guides our compassion and condemnation." We have a common moral sense when identifying whether something is morally right or wrong. This is not to say that there are no psychopaths among us, but the majority of world population utilizes a basic cache of moral guideposts. We can identify when we are doing right or wrong things. For example, if a person in the United States sees a baby on TV smiling and playing and mirrors the baby, and a person in another country, when viewing the same baby, does the same, we can conclude that we are connected with common emotional responses i.e. "We are not alone." We share basic human traits. If we entertain the proven notion that human beings across the globe have more in common than not, and pledge to treat one another the way we want to be treated, various societal ills like racism, violence, inequality, poverty and starvation will diminish over time. We humans must stand up against unfair treatment and say "yes" to diversity and inclusion, love and compassion, forgiveness, respect, and other positive energies. If we can do these things, we have made our contribution to humanity.

Consequently, if we ignore knowledge gained from this book, we have done a disservice to humanity. If we have been thinking about making a difference but did not know where to begin, "you are not alone." You have partners who are willing to join forces with you to make this world a better place, one mind at a time, one neighborhood at a time, one city at a time, one state at a time, one country at a time, and one continent at a time. Together, with positive psychology, desired thinking, altruism, empathy and love, we can improve society. In 1965, Yale psychologist Dr. Stanley Milgram was interested in measuring kindness. "He did an experiment in which he scattered stamped, addressed letters all over New Haven, dropping them onto sidewalks and placing them in telephone booths and other public places. Most letters arrived at their destinations, which means that the good people of New Haven had picked them up and put them into mailboxes—simple acts of kindness that could never be reciprocated," (Bloom, 2013). Human beings are capable of doing what is right without expecting any reward in return. If it happened in 1965, it can happen over and over again if we can translate our thoughts into actions.

Notes

Bloom, P. 2013. *Just Babies: The Origins of Good And Evil*. New York: Crown Publishing Group.

UPS (2016). UPS Delivers Unexpected and Lifesaving Wish, https://compass.ups.com/ups-driver-donates-kidney-saves-life/

Yanni Performs Live at the Acropolis, https://vimeo.com/72772866

Closing Thoughts

As we conclude this book, we hope that we have learned one or two things that could positively change the way we view our world. Hopefully, this book has helped us to understand that, whatever we expose ourselves to, we become. In other words, we become what we think and do. Because of the efficacy of what we think and how we think, we become the product of what we think about. In a thought-provoking way, we can never rise above the way we think. This book challenges us to ask thought-provoking questions. For instance, why do we think? We think because nothing ever produced was produced without a thought process. Every positive thing ever produced came into being via organized, calculated, and applied thought. Conversely, every negative thing ever produced was a result of misguided or deviant thoughts. We need to avoid questionable reputations by avoiding repetitious negative behaviors. This book aims to interrupt a pattern and develop a new way of seeing old things.

As people, we have created mental images of what human beings should look like. We have also developed certain ways of perceiving one another, particularly those who look different than us. In the process, we develop certain views about different groups of people. As a result of establishing redundant thought patterns, we tend to live in the world without considering other possibilities.

This book ventures to challenge our thoughts to entertain information from a different paradigm. This starts with self-awareness. We can begin to challenge our dogma and inadequacies. By examining our thoughts and actions, we can learn how to follow the Cloud and not the Crowd.

This book is about us loving ourselves properly. The defining word in this sentence is properly. To love ourselves properly means we will never live to hurt ourselves purposefully. And by loving ourselves properly, we reflect the same love unto others. By understanding ourselves adequately, we venture to understand one another fittingly. If we as people can understand ourselves fittingly and lovingly, we then project the same love onto others. But when the reverse is the case, we project self-loathing, resentment, biases, blame, and a host of other negative energies. By thinking through our actions and inactions, we become self-aware, and when we are self-aware, we engage with others in a more humane way.

"No man is an island." In other words, we are not alone—because what affects one directly, affects all indirectly. It is critical to know that we are never alone. We live for one another. As humans co-existing we need to live our lives through the three dimensions of a complete life. The three dimensions include loving ourselves properly; loving our neighbors; and connecting with higher power. When these three dimensions are out of order, there is turmoil. Keeping all three in harmony is the beginning of self-awareness and engagement. In all our knowing, think human. By thinking human, we begin to see all people irrespective of demographics as souls and not as suspects. As we become cognizant of the thoughts and concepts shared in this book, make efforts to apply them; we will start to experience a paradigm shift in the way we communicate with ourselves and others.

About the Authors

J. Ibeh Agbanyim, a Harvard trained leadership coaching strategist, Amazon bestselling author, public speaker, the founder of Focused Vision Consulting, LLC, has been a senior logistics associate at UPS for the past nineteen years. He is the author of The Power of Engagement, Fear, The Five Principles of Collaboration, and he contributed a chapter in a #1 Amazon international bestseller, Journeys to Success #2, inspired by the principles of Napoleon Hill. Ibeh earned a master's degree in general psychology with emphasis in industrial and organizational psychology; he is currently a PhD student in I-O psychology. Email Ibeh at powerofengagement@att.net, or website, www.fvgrowth.com

Also by J. Ibeh Agbanyim:

- Fear: *A Healthy Emotion If Well Managed*
- The Power of Engagement: *How to Find Balance in Work and Life*
- The Five Principles of Collaboration: *Applying Trust, Respect, Willingness, Empowerment, and Effective Communication to Human Relationships*
- Journeys to Success (Volume 2): *20 Empowering Stories Inspired by the Success Principles of Napoleon Hill*

Raveen Arora is an entrepreneur, author, public speaker, community cornerstone, humanitarian, professional chartered accountant, and international management consultant. He is the president/owner of India Plaza—the largest South Asian center in Arizona, home of the multi-award winning, highly-coveted Dhaba restaurant and marketplace. The center promotes Indian heritage, food, artifacts, and music. India Plaza is also a resource and educational center. Raveen is a strong community partner within the Tempe community. He has been honored multiple times at the local and national level for his lifetime of community service. He can be reached at www.thinkhuman.us, or email, arora.raveen@gmail.com

J. Ibeh Agbanyim

Index

A

acorn, 40
Albert Einstein, 1
Alex, 13
American Foundation for Suicide
Prevention, 68, 73
American Psychological Association,
23, 26, 28, 51, 57, 59
Amy Cuddy, 33, 36
Anderson, L., 83
Apache, 11
Arizona, v, vi, viii, ix, xii, xviii, 15, 36,
95
Arizona State University, viii, ix, xviii,
15

B

bias, xiii, 19, 20, 21, 22, 23, 28
Bing Li, 14
brain scan, 20
breadth of life, 68, 69, 71
Brigham, A. Bastian, 64
Brulin, C., 18

C

Cai, X. L., 9
Canada, 23
Chamberlin, J, 28
change, iii, 45, 48, 60, 61, 62, 63, 92
Charles Darwin, 34
Choon Lang Quek, 4
Chwee Beng Lee, 4
Cloud, i, 27, 30, 32, 34, 35, 93
code, 31
collaboration, vii, 58, 70
Columbia University, 77
compassion, viii, 7, 11, 15, 24, 86, 89
creative thinking, 5, 6
cremation, 84
critical thinking, iv, xv, 4, 5, 6, 80, 81
Crowd, i, 27, 30, 31, 35, 93
culture, 1, 13, 14, 17, 18, 30, 34, 85

D

Dalai Lama, xviii, 63
design thinking, 6
desire thinking, iii, 7, 9
Dhaba restaurant, 8, 95
Diversity, 7

96

www.ingramcontent.com/pod-product-compliance
Lightning Source LLC
Chambersburg PA
CBHW031520270326
41930CB00006B/459